FINDING BLISS BEYOND THE BUZZ

FROM ABUSE & ALCOHOL TO SERENITY & SOBRIETY

JANET FUGATE

Salty Sunset
Publishing

To my inner circle:
Andy, Jennifer, Lexie, Jane, Aunt J, Dad & my sweet girls.
I love you!

CONTENTS

PREFACE

First, I want to thank you for picking up my book. For the past twenty years, friends and family who know me would say, "You could write a book about all the things you've experienced in your life." It was not until I really started to accept my own story that I thought: I *can* write a book.

This book is not just a trip down memory lane but a push to assist you on your own journey to your best life. Whether you are struggling with alcohol, feeling stuck in a toxic relationship, or just needing a boost of self-confidence, my hope is that this book will support you and give you the tools you need to find your happy place. This book is sort of my way of saying "if I can do it, you can do it too." This is my attempt to share some of the wisdom I have gleaned over the years, and I hope that doing so will shorten your learning curve and encourage you not to settle.

Join me on this raw and emotional journey as I share

my experiences through an abusive marriage, a bout with cancer, the deaths of my mom and sister, my lifelong struggle with my body image, weight-loss adventure, freedom from alcohol, and my never-ending pursuit of happiness. As I bare my soul to you in the following pages, maybe you will relate to some of my experiences (hopefully not the rough parts) and decide that you, too, can change your life because, if you are reading this, it is not too late. I risk revealing myself, on a personal level, to truly accept and own my story.

I want to encourage you that, wherever you are and in whatever season of your life or situation you find yourself, there is always something to be grateful for. Bryant McGill says, "Suffering is one of life's greatest teachers." It is often out of our worst trials that our greatest victories come.

The truth is we are who we are because of what we believe and the events or experiences that have shaped our lives. We cannot control everything that happens to us, but we can decide how we will respond. Some people have extremely painful and unfortunate things happen in their lives but still feel grateful and positive. Others react to the same exact misfortune with anger and bitterness. Do you have a victim mentality or is your glass half full? I am mixing metaphors here, but the point remains. We all have a choice.

Life is fragile and precious and, while you can't change the past, you can write your own future.

"Now and then it's good to pause in our pursuit of happiness and just be happy."

— - GULLANUME APOLLINAIRE

PART I

FREEDOM FROM BONDAGE

At almost forty-five years old, I found myself lying on the cold tile bathroom floor of a mostly unfurnished one-bedroom apartment, drifting in and out of consciousness, praying I'd stop vomiting. I remember begging God not to let me die there—not because I was particularly concerned for myself but because my twenty-two-year-old daughter deserved better. Jennifer had already suffered enough through her childhood and the last thing she needed was to find her mother dead next to a toilet full of last night's red wine.

How much had I drunk? How could I let this happen? Me, Janet, the responsible one, the educated, successful healthcare executive, the level-headed, always-does-the-right-thing, money-saving, God-fearing woman who had been dutifully doing what she was supposed to do since she was twenty-one years old. Now here I was alone, drunk on the bathroom floor, separated from the man I thought was my soulmate, my husband of almost twenty-five years, my abuser. Fred was not going to make this easy. Nothing was easy with Fred.

I knew this was the most dangerous time for me. According to findings from the National Violence Against Women Survey, "men who have killed their wives indicate that either threats of separation by their partner or actual separation are most often the precipitation events that lead to the murder" (Tjaden & Thoennes, 2000). This makes sense. As the abuser begins to lose control of the victim, they become more desperate, more volatile. That was always the case with Fred. That, in part, was why this marriage had lasted nearly a quarter of a century. My previous failed attempts at leaving were always followed by even more intense suffering and fear—it was just easier to stay. His threats to kill me, Jennifer, and other family members had been believable. I knew I was in for a nasty fight, but apparently even I had a threshold for the amount of pain and abuse I could tolerate.

Needless to say, I survived that night. Unfortunately, this would not be my last toilet-hugging session. I had just escaped a very long toxic marriage. I was single, stunned, and basically just trying to survive. Alcohol became my new companion, my next abusive lover, my best friend.

"Freedom is the oxygen of the soul"

— MOSHE DAYAN

MEETING THE DEVIL

I met Fred when I was in tenth grade. It was infatuation at first sight. We met at my part-time job at a portrait sales company; my job was to call and sell the portrait packages and Fred's job was to drive to the customers' homes and deliver the certificates. Today, this seems like an antiquated way of doing business, but there were no cell phones at the time and the internet did not yet exist. It was indeed a different time. The first day I met Fred, I was smitten. I think it was his baby blue eyes, jet black hair, and bad boy smile that drew me in. It didn't hurt that he had a nice tan and drove a cool convertible. All of the other high school girls working there thought he was dreamy, and I couldn't believe my luck when I was the one that ended up in his car headed for a day at the beach just a few weeks later.

There were red flags from the first day I met him, but I plunged ahead thinking I was deeply in love with this hot mess of a man. We dated off and on for almost a year. I was miserable when we weren't together. When we finally got together for good, he was driving a beater car—the cool convertible had been wrecked by that point—he had no money, no job, no driver's license, no car insurance, and nowhere to live. He ended up moving in with me at my mom's house. I found out he had been married for a short period of time and was attending mandatory spouse-abuse classes. If that isn't a red flag, I don't know what is.

By all accounts he was a total loser, but I thought I was in love—or maybe I thought he needed me and I could help him. Whatever it was, there is no rational explanation for what possessed me to think marrying Fred was a good idea, but that is exactly what I did. I was nineteen years old and hell-bent on marrying this man. Maybe he only married me because I was working, had a decent car and a place to live. Or maybe it was more malicious and he married me because I was an easy target to torment and control. It all seems quite bizarre and erratic, but at the time, I couldn't see anything but him.

My parents and sister tried to talk me out of it. My friends begged me not to do it. I wouldn't listen to reason. I remember spending the night with my best friend a few weeks before the wedding. She'd asked, "Why are you marrying Fred?" She continued to question my judgment. I recall admitting that, logically, she was right and that it made no sense, but I could not control my heart. Looking back, I wonder if I was flattered that someone I thought was so attractive and desired by other women would want me. My low self-esteem was obviously a driving factor. I was in lust or love or something, but whatever it was it was powerful, and I couldn't stop it.

In the fall after I graduated high school, I was married.

Fred and I had no money, so I borrowed a wedding dress, made hand-written wedding invitations, and rented him a baby blue tuxedo. The simple ceremony was held at my mom's house. No one in attendance expected this marriage to last six months, and deep down that probably included me too.

But here I was, nearly twenty-five years later, still desperately trying to get over my obsession with Fred. It is very painful to recall all of the suffering of those years and I am filled with sadness for wasting my youth and living in this vicious cycle of domestic abuse. Throughout the years, I tried to leave many times, but every time the threats, fear, and promises of changing sucked me back in. But I finally did it—I'd left him.

Once our daughter Jennifer was grown and moved out of the house, the fights with Fred escalated. My tolerance of the control and abuse were coming to an end and I started standing up to him. The more I stood up for myself, the more violent he became. Surely, he was sensing that he was losing control. I was so tired of living in fear, walking on eggshells, and enduring this abuse. It was getting more and more difficult for me to want to keep the peace. One day— I really don't even know what triggered it—I had had enough. We got into an argument. He yelled at me about some trivial matter and, surprisingly, I screamed back. I think he was shocked, but it really made him angry and he picked up a handheld back massager and threw it at me. It hit me in the chest before falling to the ground. My instincts kicked in and, for the first time ever, I fought back—I picked it up and threw it back at him. That was it. He raged at me in a way I had never seen. I was trying to get to the back bedroom away

7

from him when he caught up to me. He knocked me to the ground and I started kicking. Fighting back was so uncharacteristic of me. In all of the previous attacks, I would cower and cover my face and head, trying to avoid or lessen the blows. I was sure he was going to kill me.

As I laid on the floor in the hall, he picked up a huge planter. It was filled with dirt and a massive corn plant. He raised it over my head. I ducked, covered my head, and prepared for the impact, but he threw it beside me and stormed away. I jumped up and ran as fast as I could to my bedroom closet to get my purse and car keys. I rushed past him digging in his closet. Then, he pulled out what he had been searching for—his gun. I was on the floor gathering my items, but before I knew it, he was standing over me in my closet, pointing the gun at my head. I was trembling and shaking, the rush of emotions and fight-or-flight hormones racing through my body. At that moment, I felt like death would be preferable to continuing to live life this way, and I screamed, "Just do it!" I had nearly resigned myself to the idea that I would never be free from him and he would likely kill me sooner or later anyway. Fred shot the gun at the floor. I screamed and he calmly handed the gun to me. "Go ahead and kill me," he said. I thought long and hard about pulling the trigger. Even as I sat there quivering with fear and anger, adrenaline surging, I knew I could never do it. After what seemed like an eternity, he took the gun out of my hand. He said, "You just want me to kill myself, don't you?" Stress hormones filled my throat and paralyzed my vocal cords. I could not respond. I watched him put the gun to his head. Deep down I suspected that I really did want him to die because I honestly believed it was the only way this suffering would ever truly end. He didn't pull the trigger, and somehow in my stupor I managed to get my car keys and run out of the house.

Fred had already destroyed so many of my precious possessions. During my last attempt to leave him, I only took what I could fit in my friend's van and he burned everything else I had—letters from my deceased mom, photo albums, yearbooks, and my favorite childhood stuffed animal. I went to Jennifer's house and told her what had happened. We called the police and took pictures of the bruises. Nothing would come of it. It seemed like nothing ever did.

I was afraid, but I knew I couldn't go back this time. I thought about all the victims who had made this exact decision and didn't live to tell their story. I worried he would kill me and then kill himself. Murder-suicide was something Fred had threatened often over the years, and I knew leaving him was risky, but staying was even more dangerous. I had to get out.

Getting help was critical. I called the National Domestic Violence Hotline and they told me where to go to file a restraining order. I was finally going to stand up for myself. Entering the courthouse, my heart began to race. Armed guards and policemen without smiles greeted me at the metal detector. As I handed over my purse to be searched and prepared for my walk through the machine, I tried to smile at the officer. Without making eye contact he asked what I was there for and in the middle of the open corridor with people all around I had to explain my need for a restraining order. The courthouse is an intimidating place. Regardless of why you are there, it seems so formal and threatening. A place to get protection, I suppose, but I got the feeling everyone entering was suspect. The intake questioning felt very invasive and a couple of times I thought about just walking out. The clerk was no less frightening and when he asked his questions there was a tone of disbelief in his voice. "When did the incident happen and have you reported it before?" I am sure the staff has seen and heard it all and become a bit jaded from having to see humanity at its worst day after day. After answering the questions, apparently with the right answers, I was relieved to finally be granted a temporary restraining order and put "into the system." I was told to keep a copy with me at all times and to call the police and show them the paperwork if Fred came near me.

The bruises healed quickly, as they usually did, and then my new reality set in—I didn't have a home anymore, only the clothes on my back. My whole life as I'd known it was gone and would never be the same again. I realize now that I'd been brainwashed. How had I let this happen? Was I really that weak? As I researched narcissism and read about domestic violence, it all became more and more clear. The abuser isolates their victim and feeds them streams of negativity. They use creative techniques like gaslighting and manipulation. Most of these people are so good at their skill, you don't even know what hit you. Dealing with low self-image and hooking up with someone who wants to control you is a disastrous combination. Being young and vulnerable is also very helpful. I became dependent on him in that I was so focused on trying to keep peace and please him that I didn't really exist. Being continually called fat, ugly, and stupid has a profound effect on your perception of yourself. When the one you vowed to love forever, who you trusted with your heart and who knows your most intimate secrets, turns from lover to enemy, it is vicious. The offender understands where you are most vulnerable and uses that to keep you down, afraid, controlled, and dependent upon them.

When I finally started pursuing a divorce and opened up to a few people, a friend gave me a book, *Women that Love Too Much* by Robin Norwood. It was a game changer. I saw myself on every page. I was addicted to him. I was so busy trying to fix him and make him happy that I had completely lost myself. I was not alone. I could relate so well with the stories and characters in that book. It was so eye opening. I also learned about gaslighting. Dr. Sarkis describes it like this:

> *Gaslighting is a tactic in which a person or entity, in order to gain more power, makes a victim question their reality. It works much better than you may think. Anyone is susceptible to gaslighting, and it is a common technique of abusers, dictators, narcissists, and cult leaders. It is done slowly, so the victim doesn't realize how much they've been brainwashed. For example, in the movie* Gaslight *(1944), a man manipulates his wife to the point where she thinks she is losing her mind. (Sarkis, 2003)*

So that's what it's called? Fred often told me that what I had just experienced didn't really happen and that I was crazy. Try living in that for more than twenty years. Actually, if you can help it, don't! I was convinced my memory was bad and questioned my own sanity. When I finally read about gaslighting and realized that it was what I had been experiencing, it was a huge relief, a realization of just how deluded I'd been.

I want to stop here in my story to say this—if you are in an abusive relationship, now is the time to get out! No matter what you are being told, no one deserves to be hit, kicked, spit on, slapped, or choked—*not even once*. No one deserves that. The National Coalition Against Domestic Violence shares an alarming statistic: "On average, nearly 20 people per minute are physically abused by an intimate partner in the United States. In a single year, this equates to more than ten million women and men" (National Coalition Against Domestic Violence, 2011). You only have one life, and life is short, so please get help now. There is a list of resources, tips, and contacts in the appendix. No matter what it takes, removing yourself and your children from an abusive situation is the right thing to do. Life is short! Please don't waste twenty-five years like I did. The longer you wait, the harder it gets to leave.

"What will you do with your one wild and precious life?"
—Mary Oliver

BY DAY, I was the COO at a reputable healthcare organization. I really loved my job. I poured my heart and soul into the company, and it provided me with an outlet for my time and energy. The physicians I worked with were the best in the business. I was proud to be a part of making it possible for their life-saving skills to flourish in a well-run clinic. The CEO, Chuck, who had hired me, was my mentor and had become my friend. He taught me how to handle the physicians in the boardroom and helped me tone down my passion when I felt someone was being treated unfairly. A large part of my job was listening to the physicians' operational concerns and improving personnel and processes. I was really good in my role. Being a registered nurse gave me a bit of credibility with physicians and clinical staff, and that was one thing Chuck didn't have. Chuck was an accountant and much less touchy feely than me. Together we were a great team. I recruited Lexie to come help me manage the operations. I also met Sophie and ToriJill. These ladies would end up playing a crucial role in my journey through the divorce and become lifelong friends.

When I left Fred, I moved closer to my job. My separation and divorce were playing out publicly in front of the entire company and it was not pretty. I imagine that most mornings I looked like hell, with swollen eyes, puffy face, and slapped-on makeup. It was fortunate for me that I had been working with Chuck and the doctors for some time before this happened. They all knew it was not characteristic of me and that I was just going through a rough time. My assistant Penny was a beautiful girl. She was super smart and capable. Many days immediately after the separation, I would go into my office, shut the door, and just cry. Penny would come in and help me organize the day. She fielded calls and handled all the minor things she could manage without me. Fred called my job incessantly harassing me and anyone who would answer the phone, despite the restraining order. He made every attempt to humiliate me. One day, Fred emailed a nude photo of me to Chuck. He was stupid enough to tell me and I immediately had IT block his account. You can imagine that awkward conversation, with both the IT director and my boss. I remember calling the police and reporting yet another violation of the restraining order.

No wonder so many women stay in abusive relationships—law enforcement really can't do much until you actually get hurt, and often, by then, it's too late. I remember going to my hairdresser Wendy during this tenuous time and confiding in her about my situation. There was another hairdresser, Linda, working in the small shop. Wendy told me Linda was in a similar situation and asked if she could include her in the conversation. Linda was an older lady, attractive in her own way, but the life of pain had clearly taken a toll on her. She told me her own story about leaving her violent husband a few weeks earlier. She told me how happy she was for the first time in many years and encouraged me to get away from Fred while I was still young.

All things are relative. About five weeks later, when I went back to see Wendy, she immediately gave me a hug and started crying. She said, "I have been so worried about you. Linda is dead. Her husband killed her, then he killed himself." I couldn't believe it. Yes, I had seen the story on the news, but I didn't realize it was Linda. I thought about her kind smile and sincere pleading for me to get out of my situation. Now she was dead. Wendy and I talked about Linda's daughter and her grandchildren. I cried and cried. I cried for her, for the injustice of it all, and I cried for myself out of fear. I became more aware of my surroundings and vowed to be diligent reporting his actions to the police.

A police officer was sent to my place of employment. Just what every organization wants, law enforcement being summoned to their place of business. The young policeman sat down in my office across from my desk. He went through the formalities of my complaint. I presented my restraining order against Fred, which clearly said no contact with me. He was not supposed to come near me or contact me, my workplace, or any of my family. This paperwork meant nothing to Fred. I guess, in fairness, he had played this scenario out many times before. My previous attempted separation looked eerily similar.

Flashback to a previous time when I'd left and he'd begun threatening to come to my workplace and kill everyone. The employees had been scared to death. The physician suggested we cancel patients and close the office. The outrageous phone calls and vulgar voicemails were like scenes of an episode of *Snapped* and no one else working there had ever seen anyone in real life so aggressive and angry. I'd felt bad. The profanity and intimidation were all too familiar to me, but it had caused all this disturbance to my employer and fellow staff members; they didn't deserve that. I'd ended up going back to Fred, ending that office drama.

That was not the first time I'd gone back, and I'm certain he thought this time would be no different. The officer wrote out his report and then said quite matter-of-factly and without expression, "I need to see the picture." My heart sunk, and I wanted to crawl under my desk and cry. More humiliation, more abuse. I pulled up the image on my computer. He walked past my desk to get a closer look then asked me to zoom in a little to confirm that it was me in the photo. Filled with numbness, I complied. I was used to doing things that I didn't want to do. I was used to being told what to do. I was familiar with being controlled. He saw my embarrassment and smiled. "You have nothing to be embarrassed about Janet, you didn't do anything wrong." Yeah right, dude, you are not the one showing a total stranger of the opposite sex a half-naked picture of yourself, I thought to myself. I hung my head a little and knew this was only the beginning of the agony I was going to endure to escape this marriage. The officer thanked me and left. There was no reassurance that I would be protected or that Fred would be held accountable, just a free peek of my boobs and another stab at my dignity.

I HADN'T LIVED in an apartment in over twenty years, but there I was in the top floor unit staring at the empty walls and wondering how I would survive. At least I didn't have any financial concerns. I had been the breadwinner in my family for many years, with Fred in and out of treatment centers and barely working throughout most of our marriage. I had put myself through school while I worked full time. First nursing school—it took me almost four years to complete the two-year degree program. The only time I cut back to part time was when I started my nursing clinicals, and I picked up weekend shifts at the hospital as a monitor tech to compensate. I was the first person in my immediate family to graduate college, so it was a big deal. My mom and dad hadn't gone to college and there was little talk about me going. I graduated high school and got a job like everyone else in my circle. I took a few college classes here and there, but when I got married at nineteen and had Jennifer four years later, that pretty much ended any further thoughts of higher education.

Most of my career, if you want to call it that, was working in physician offices. My senior year of high school, I was in a business program where I went to school for half the day and worked the other half. I was a receptionist at a physician's practice, a position I kept after graduation. I went on to work in several different departments and positions, advancing to insurance clerk, billing specialist, and then manager. By the time I became a nurse, I'd become familiar with every position in a physician's office.

I worked a couple years as a floor nurse on the night shift. It was horrible—not the nursing part—but I never could adjust to the sleep deficit. I would work a twelve-hour shift, drive home exhausted and sleep eight hours, only to wake up still unrested. When a physician approached me about managing his practice, I jumped at the opportunity and never really looked back. Now, in addition to the administrative side of running the clinic, I also knew the clinical roles as well. Not long after, I left hospital nursing and went back to school to earn my bachelor's degree. I'd always been a hard worker, eager to learn and grow. I recall having to write my career goals in my undergraduate degree program and I wrote that I wanted to be the COO of a cardiology physician's practice, and a few years later that is exactly what I'd become. I think, as I advanced my education and grew more successful in my career, I began to doubt some of the constant lies Fred had been telling me for all those years. I began to question how I could be stupid and incompetent yet pass college courses with flying colors and have glowing reviews on annual work assessments. Something wasn't adding up. Maybe I wasn't as stupid, lazy, and worthless as he'd insisted I was.

FREEDOM WAS SCARY, but it was also exhilarating. I was on my own for the first time—ever! Alcohol was there to see me through. I began to make friends and go out. I had never really done much of that. I had missed the traditional partying of college days and the period of discovering what you like and who you are. I went straight from my parents' house to my husband's. I knew I was a social person and loved being around people. I have no idea how I was able to cope with being so isolated with just Fred all those years. Being away from oppression and control left me vulnerable and so very empty. Who am I? What does Janet like? I knew what Fred liked and that had basically become what I liked, but now I had the opportunity to figure out what I liked and learn about me. I made a lot of friends. I discovered going out to bars, dancing, and having a blast. I had parties and surrounded myself with people. If I was busy and distracted with friends, I didn't have to miss my house or my marital status. On the occasional night when I had nothing planned, I would sit in my lonely apartment and turn to my other best friend and coping mechanism, red wine. It was working overtime and so was I. I devoted even more time to my job. I was at every late-night recruitment dinner, investment talk, and board meeting. My position had always been important to me, but now it was my lifeline, my identity.

By surrounding myself with a small circle of trust—my daughter Jennifer, my best friend Lexie, my pastor, my therapist and a few close friends—I started to share what was happening. Everyone except my daughter, of course, was shocked that I had been living in this nightmare. I would recount a story or share something Fred had said to me, and my friends were surprised and disgusted. They would ask me, "How could he talk to you like that?" The next embarrassing part was admitting that I had tolerated and accepted this debasement.

There is a role in the domestic abuse cycle that the victim plays, and that is to keep quiet. I didn't tell anyone. If you are not going to leave, how can you share how terrible it is? "Get out or shut up" is kind of the unspoken rule. I covered for his bad behavior and bailed him out more times than I care to admit. After all those years, I was tired of the lies, I was tired of pretending. Pretending my life was okay, my marriage was good, and my husband didn't emotionally and physically abuse me. The other realization was that his horrible words were what I heard and believed in my own mind, even when he wasn't saying them. I was so conditioned and had heard them so much that I believed them. "I am worthless. I am unable to do anything on my own. No one will ever love me. I make stupid decisions. I don't have enough sense to live on my own (without him). I don't deserve anything good." And the list goes on.

Something didn't add up for me: how could I be all

those horrible things Fred described but still have managed to do so many great things? I had put myself through school while working full time and caring for the house, him, and Jennifer. I had advanced my career and people at work thought I was smart and quite capable. Something had to be wrong. How could I have such success at work yet be such a useless dumbass? It didn't make sense, but his opinion mattered more than mine or anyone else's.

I recall wearing a dress to work one day. It was a simple, but pretty dress. I obviously liked it. When I got to work, I received a lot of compliments about my outfit, but when I went home, Fred looked at me and said, "Did you wear that to work?"

I said, "Yes, do you like it?"

He replied, "You look like shit in that dress. I can't believe you actually wore it out of the house."

I threw the dress away. The reality was I didn't even have a clear understanding of who I really was. I viewed myself through Fred's eyes, with disdain and disgust. Anytime I had an accomplishment or an event that would even slightly build me up, he would quickly smash it down with his jaded view of the situation. When I came home with news of a pay raise or bonus, he belittled the amount and would say, "You should have asked for more."

Eventually, as the scales of reality began tipping, I started getting glimpses of self-worth and recognizing that some of the outlandish things he said about me were blatant lies. I even began questioning why he would want to stay with someone he hated so much. He always replied, "I am committed until death do us part—as God ordained." Those words haunted me.

. . .

AS I BEGAN SHARING my secret life and opening up to my inner circle of trust, it became clear that I could not even trust my own thoughts. Now that is a scary place to be! I would literally have to call one of my confidants and ask if I was making a good decision. It was an uphill battle with me listening to his crazy pleas and trying his outright best to get me back under control. He went to great lengths to keep his voice in my head. He threatened murder, suicide, humiliation, financial ruin, and hell fire. His favorite tactic was to try to convince me I was going to Hell and that God would reject me, eternally, if I didn't honor our marriage vows. He would say, "In God's eyes we are married for life." It is certainly an interesting strategy for him to have used considering he'd previously been married.

I WENT to therapy twice a week. I took a divorce care class. I bought every book I could find about domestic violence, codependence, and surviving a divorce. Oh, and I drank. I drank a lot, but I also worked very hard on my recovery. I wanted to be whole. I did not even know how broken I was. I remember my best friend, Lexie, telling me that she could not wait until I could see myself like everyone else did. I had no earthly idea what that meant. It must have been a bit shocking to learn that your boss, who was extremely decisive, intelligent, and effective at work, lived such a disparate life at home.

. . .

THE DIVORCE WAS NOT a quick process. Fred continued to act out and hid from law enforcement when they tried to serve him the divorce papers. The only reason they were able to present him with the papers was because I knew he had to go to court on the charge of violating the restraining order and I called the courthouse. I pleaded with them to serve him the divorce papers while he was there and, thankfully, they complied. It still took well over a year to finalize the divorce. In the meantime, the limbo and the harassment continued.

MY ATTORNEY WAS no match for the powerful divorce attorney Fred sprang for. Mine just kept saying, "You just want to get him out of your life. Nothing else matters." He told me this divorce could drag on for years and I honestly didn't think I could survive.

At mediation, I started with fair—offering Fred half of the house, half of the money, and one of the vehicles. He, on the other hand, demanded the house, everything in it, all the money, and he wanted me to pay him alimony and provide him health insurance. I thought when the mediator told me of Fred's demands that I might have a stroke right then and there. In what kind of world does a person endure years of mental and physical torment, finally escape, and then find themselves required to pay the abuser? I had no doubt he was telling his female attorney a very different version of the truth. He was the victim— he was always the victim. In his personal fiction, he had sacrificed and put me through school and supported me, and now that I had an education and career, I was leaving him. He deserved compensation.

In the end, the compromise was I didn't pay alimony and he got just about everything else. Honestly, I still got the better deal. I got my life back.

THE DAY of the actual divorce, I was scared to death. I thought for sure he was going to bring a gun and kill me. Ironically, after the proceeding, I was in my car and a truck pulled up beside me. It was Fred and his friend. He yelled something about me being lucky he didn't kill me today. The restraining order with the divorce papers ended a year later, but his harassment didn't. He has literally contacted every employer I have had since I left him. He messaged me as recently as six months ago. The harassment and stalking never end.

FRED CONTACTED me at one of my positions and left urgent messages. He just kept calling and asking for me, until someone finally got me on the phone. When I answered, he said, "This is your husband. You know we are still married in God's eyes."

I was shaking inside, but managed to say, "Fred, what do you want?"

He just started with his usual slander. "You're such a whore, you bitch, you . . ." and I hung up the phone.

The next time he called I had one of my friends answer and tell him that I had called the police and if he didn't want to go to jail, he had better stop calling. At another job of mine, he posted a disparaging comment on the company Facebook page. Someone called to let me know, and they were able to get the comment deleted. It was embarrassing to have to explain my crazy ex-husband story; even though everyone seems to be very sympathetic, I wondered if it accomplished Fred's goal and tainted their opinion of me. Another time, Fred called the human resources manager and left a voicemail telling them why they should not employ me. He included a whole bunch of derogatory remarks about my character. Then there was the call when he found out about my sister. The number was blocked and I reluctantly answered. As soon as I heard his voice I felt sick.

I said "Fred what do you want? Why don't you leave me alone?

He said, "I heard CC is dying?

I responded, "yes, what do you want?"

He callously said, "I can't wait until you and every one of your family members dies of cancer."

I just hung up. This call didn't surprise me it was what I had come to expect. Kick me when I am down. After my sister's death he had enough nerve to call my dad to offer his condolences. Really?

I could go on and on.

EIGHT YEARS AFTER OUR DIVORCE, he found my rental website. Of course, my phone number was listed. He began calling me hundreds of times a day, leaving disturbing and deranged messages. He started posting negative comments and lies on my business site. I went to file another restraining order and was connected with a free attorney who handled domestic violence cases. She was wonderful, a real godsend. Our divorce was so many years ago, yet here he was actively haunting me. He threatened to come to our daughter's wedding (although he was not invited) and said things like, "I know where you are, and I will see you soon." It was terrifying!

I HAVE a large file with all the messages, transcribed calls, and contacts he has made. I downloaded all the voicemails and brought them to the sheriff and my appointed attorney. My attorney said she had done over a thousand cases of domestic abuse and this was one of the worst she had ever seen. I don't know if I should have been flattered or outraged.

The day of court, he said he was going to be there but then asked to be called instead. The judge tried his number and no one answered. He listened to the case my attorney presented, including one of the bizarre and threatening voicemails, asked me a couple of questions, then granted me a permanent restraining order. That was in 2015, and since then I have reported several more violations. A couple of warrants have been issued for his arrest, but nothing has happened. Honestly, I just want him to leave me alone. I hate to say it, but I don't think I'll truly be free of him until one of us dies. I just hope that, if I die first, it's not at his hand. I can only imagine his reaction to this book, but I refuse to be silenced by fear any longer.

IF MY STORY helps one person decide to leave an abusive situation, it will have been worth the struggle. I am grateful I am alive to tell my story because I know so many others who were not as lucky.

. . .

THERE ARE a lot of regrets regarding this chapter in my life. I should have left sooner. I should have protected my child better. I wasted my youth and so much of my life living in this horrific situation. I cannot change the past, but I can choose not to dwell on it. We all have choices to make: stay the victim and be angry or bitter about what has happened to you or move forward and live the best life you can possibly live now.

I don't hate him.

I've let go of the anger. Holding onto it is like drinking poison and hoping the other person dies.

I am so thankful that I am free. Free to be imperfect me.

THE EARLY DAYS

*L*et me back up a bit and tell you about my younger years and my first experience with alcohol. I was maybe twelve years old. My parents had gone out and I decided to get into their vodka stash. I have no idea how much I drank, but the story goes that when they got home, I was staggering around, slurring my words. They asked me what had happened, and I guess I could not come up with a lucid answer. When they pressed me on why their vodka bottle was empty, my famous reply was, "Someone must have come in and drank it." I was obviously in big trouble. Despite feeling bad, I didn't even throw up. Apparently I had a tolerance from early on. I didn't continue drinking at age twelve, but I do remember it didn't seem all that bad.

My parents drank socially, but neither of them was a daily drinker. As a kid, I never saw either of them drunk. We were Baptists. You may have heard the joke about the difference between seeing a Baptist and seeing a Presbyterian in the liquor store: the Presbyterian speaks.

Baptists frown on drinking and, as a child, I was taught alcohol was taboo and should be avoided. I have vague memories of my mom and dad at their friend's house, me playing with the other kids and the older kids talking about sneaking a drink, but I never had. My maternal grandma and grandpa were not drinkers, at least as far as I knew. They attended the Baptist church every Sunday and, if they did drink, it was on the down low. I never met my dad's parents—they both died before I was born—but they both drank. A lot. Both of my dad's brothers were alcoholics. I loved my uncles, but once they crossed a certain line, they were either escorted home or my sister and I were shooed off to bed. I was often warned in my youth about having the alcoholic gene. My dad also said he didn't drink much because he saw what it did to his mom, dad, and brothers. Interesting how kids either emulate their parents or become hellbent not to be like them. I am very grateful he chose the latter.

My family moved to Jacksonville, Florida, when I was eleven years old. It was difficult for me at first, but Jacksonville would become my hometown. Adjusting to life in Jacksonville must have been difficult for all of us. My dad left my mom about a year after we moved there. I was thirteen years old and immediately fast-tracked from teenager to becoming an adult. I thought their separation was the most bizarre and unexpected thing that could have happened. I never once heard my parents argue. I thought they had a great marriage. They didn't divorce until many, many years later. I guess the reason my dad decided to leave added to the agony. My dad was my mom's only. He was her world. My sister CC once said my mom loved him too much. Looking back, I don't disagree. My dad played in a country band and that is where he met his mistress.

Bertha was "a friend," and she, my mom, and my dad spent plenty of time together. Bertha was the singer in the band and also played the guitar. We all knew her, as she had been to the house many times. I guess my dad was smitten with her blond beehive, skinny figure, and long painted nails. Bertha was the exact opposite of mom in almost every way. The physical was blatantly obvious, with Bertha being tall, thin, and heavily made up. My mom was more of a natural beauty with flowing black hair, hazel eyes, and the warmest, most inviting smile. She was overweight and had, indeed, struggled with her weight her entire life. Still, she was a beautiful lady with a curvy, full-figured shape. Okay, I could be a little biased here, but seriously my mom was very attractive. Deep down, I always believed my dad left mom because she was fat. I don't know if this caused my body image issues, but I am positive it didn't help. Bertha smoked cigarettes, wore tight jeans and high heels. I could not believe my dad would choose a woman like that over my mom. One day he announced he was moving out. It wasn't until a few weeks later we learned he was moving in with Bertha. It was a BAD scene! My sister and I were eyewitnesses to the end of a very tragic love story.

My codependent mother became suicidal and began drinking her pain away every night. Her anger and rage for Bertha was uncontrollable. She did some crazy things in those first few years. I remember my mom having me or my sister call Bertha's house and ask for my dad. When he would get on the phone, my mom would take the receiver and proceed to bitch him out about one thing or another. One time she drove to Bertha's house, and I am not exactly sure what happened, but my dad came out, words were exchanged, then one thing led to another, a shot was fired, and there was a hole in the floorboard of our family station wagon. There were lots of calls to Bertha cussing at her and calling her names. My dad tried to keep the peace, but I am confident neither lady was all too happy.

CC and I missed him a lot at first, but we quickly adopted our mother's fury toward the woman who had wrecked our home. Looking back, as an adult, it is probably a miracle that Bertha didn't kick my dad out or have my mom arrested. The harassment was relentless. I guess my dad felt guilty, but he'd made his decision. It was impossible for me to understand his motives, perhaps because he didn't know himself. Maybe his love for Bertha was so powerful and all-consuming or maybe he was just over being married to my mom. Neither of these seemed an acceptable reason to leave your children and family. I wanted to understand why, I wanted something or someone other than him to blame. It wasn't a quick and easy escape for him and the angry part of me didn't care. Dad was so worried that Mom was going to kill herself, he didn't even mention a divorce. Instead of ripping off the Band-Aid, divorcing, and ending all contact, there were many years where my dad would come and play house with us. He spent most holidays with "his family."

CC and I watched the passive aggressive love/hate relationship between my mom and dad for years. My mom wanted to die. I watched her cry herself to sleep most nights after polishing off a bottle of cheap wine. I saw her threaten to take too many sleeping pills. Once I walked into her bedroom and she had a gun to her head. I can't describe how I felt other than helpless. I kept saying "Mom, you still have me and CC." It was clear that we were not enough at that time. She couldn't see past her pain and grief. My poor sister was really like a lost child. I became my mom's caretaker and confidant, and CC . . . well, she just survived. As a mother myself today, I see how sick and selfish her actions were. Yet, it doesn't make me love her any less. I understand, first hand, how you can be so caught up in your own pain or fear that you don't see what is really happening around you. It is impossible to realize what's important. I live as a mother with my own regrets. I watched my mom use alcohol to cope with her pain. Years later, I found myself doing the same.

My comfortless mom kept trying to get my dad back. I think she would have done anything. The desperation was pitiful. My dad felt pity, but no love. My sister learned from watching and determined at an early age that she would never love anyone as much as my mom loved my dad. She vowed she would never let anyone close enough to hurt her like that and she never did. CC had a lot of boyfriends and lovers, but if any of them got too close she pushed them away. She always said she was waiting for the right one to come along. She admitted that she picked losers (which she did), but I think deep down she was determined not to allow herself to be as vulnerable as my mom was.

. . .

WITHOUT WARNING, when I was in tenth grade, I started having panic attacks. Of course, I had no idea what they were. I thought something bad was happening to me. Truth is, something bad *was* happening to me! My desperate mom frantically took me to all kinds of physicians for every possible test. There had to be an explanation for these horrible events. If you have never experienced a panic attack, first of all, good for you. I would describe the feeling as a sudden onset of intense fear. You feel powerless to cope, explain, or communicate what is happening to you. It is terrifying. After tons of tests and exams, the diagnosis was that it was nothing physical. "Oh great," I thought, "it *is* mental. I'm crazy."

The panic attacks were so bad I couldn't go to school. I didn't want to leave the house. I failed an entire semester of school because I couldn't attend classes. There was no grace for anyone suffering with mental health issues back then. CC was once again shuffled to the back burner while resources and time were spent trying to help me. I was referred to a child psychologist. I remember the poster in his waiting room. It was a picture of a beautiful sunset that said, "The sun will set without thy assistance." This is a truth that I sometimes still struggle with. Feeling responsible for everyone and worrying about everything can be daunting. I guess it's in my DNA. At five years old, I had overheard my mom and dad discussing some financial difficulties about not having the money to pay the bills or buy groceries. I became so worried and concerned, the story has it, that I started crying and asked them how we were going to get our next loaf of bread? Perhaps that is why I never heard them argue or fight. Maybe they were trying to protect me from my incessant worry. Worry would be another lifelong challenge I would need to cope with and address.

Counseling was a godsend and, although my psychologist was my polar opposite, he was able to reach me. A simple trick of breathing and watching the clock for a minute tamed my anxiety attacks. Perhaps once I knew what was happening to me, I was better able to deal with it. He basically said that, because I had to hold myself and everyone around me together during the traumatic time when my dad had left, so many months later after things had calmed down my body was responding to the crisis event. Seemed reasonable.

After a month or so of weekly visits, he cut my appointments down to biweekly, then to monthly, and then one day told me I didn't need to come back. It was a bittersweet day. I was glad I was "cured," but I was going to miss our talks. It would be many, many years later before I found my way back into therapy. I think, if money was no object, it would be a weekly ritual. Who couldn't benefit from a professional, unbiased listener in their life? I feel fortunate this positive experience gave me a foundation with counseling so that later in life, when I needed help, I wasn't afraid to seek it out. It is quite sad that our society has not been able to do away with the stigma of mental health issues. So many people suffer needlessly because they are afraid, embarrassed, or unable to reach out for help.

I FOUND alcohol as a faithful companion around my junior year in high school. I experimented with marijuana and did my fair share, but drinking was my jam. I remember getting drunk with friends in high school. I had a few friends but never really felt like I fit in. I was always counting down the days till I'd be done with school. I was an okay student and good grades were relatively effortless for me. I managed to pass my sophomore year even though I had failed every class the semester of my panic attacks, but thankfully I was able to work hard, ace the next semester, and pass for the year with Cs. By eleventh grade, I was academically back on track and managed to make honor roll. I maintained good grades through my senior year and even joined Future Business Leaders of America. My mom had one goal for me and CC, and that was to graduate high school. She banged on our bedroom doors every morning, screamed, begged, and pushed us to get through school. No matter what else was happening in our lives, failing or quitting school was not an option.

IT REALLY WAS KIND OF like the perfect storm for a hormonal teenager to be paired with a heartbroken mother who could barely function. By the time I was sixteen, it was a free for all. My mom/friend was now partying with me. She was by far the coolest mom on the block and the envy of all my friends. In reality, she was a middle-aged woman dejected by the love of her life, drowning her pain with booze and men. My mom was too broken and needy to parent me or my sister. I would come home late at night after a night of drinking and partying with friends to find that her there partying with some friends of her own or still out. She brought a lot of creepy guys home. Some even made passes at me or my little sister. The seventies were a crazy time in general. Lots of free love, doing what felt good, and being groovy. Women's rights, liberation, and equality issues were front and center. It would be easy to judge our promiscuity, but it was quite normal for that decade. I am neither excusing nor blaming my mom, who I love dearly, simply explaining how things lined up for me then.

WHEN YOU LOOK BACK over your life, you no doubt see the events with different filters and life wisdom. I have spent plenty of money on therapy and self-help examining the aftermath of my childhood, but I don't consider myself a victim. My parents made choices that had consequences for themselves and their children, as we all do. We made our peace with that tumultuous time in our lives. As adults we discussed these events, and my mom apologized profusely more than once for her neglectful state. Of course, I've forgiven her—she's my mom! Even writing this now gives me pause because I don't want to paint my parents in a bad light.

Perhaps I am an apologist, but life is too short to be stuck in the past that cannot be changed. My mom was my best friend. She and I shared such a strong connection. I always knew she was my biggest fan. I didn't realize until I had my own daughter how she literally felt every one of my pains or failures and celebrated every single positive move or success. She was in many ways, despite her weaknesses, the strongest woman I have ever known. After my dad left and she stabilized, she worked two jobs, took in roommates, and did whatever she had to do to provide for her girls. My mom never met a stranger and was always bringing stray people in. Most Thanksgivings, Christmases, and many other times for no reason, she would have people at our table who were lonely or needed help. She was loving and giving. My mom surrounded herself with friends and family. Her laugh was as infectious as her smile and her heart was as big as they come. She was an amazing mother and grandmother, and I still miss her every single day.

MY DAD and Bertha are still married to this day. I am very thankful that he has had someone to love and support him through all these years. Guess you never really know how a single decision, good or bad, can change your life and the lives of many of those around you forever.

SAVING GRACE

*I*n my early twenties, I found myself in a very difficult marriage working a dead-end job with no college education. I was drinking, smoking, and struggling through life. I was already tired of the way things were going. I am sure I was searching for something.

Fred's sister Sherry invited me to go to an evangelistic meeting. I was raised a Baptist but probably hadn't been to church since I was maybe twelve years old. My mom always took me and my sister to Sunday school and church. My grandfather was the church custodian and I attended church with the family every Sunday as far back as I can remember—it was our ritual. I think my mom quit going once my sister and I were old enough to say we did not want to go. Even with all the church attendance and being baptized at a young age, I didn't really know what the Bible said, just what I had been told.

I didn't accept Sherry's invitation at first. Then, one Saturday afternoon, Fred and I had spent the day at the beach. I had been drinking the entire time and I am positive he was smoking weed and indulging in some other recreational drugs. Anyway, we came home from the beach, had sex, and passed out. This was not uncommon for us. Then I had a dream. It was a very real, very vivid dream. I will never forget it.

In my dream, I heard a knocking noise coming from the air conditioning closet in the apartment. I got up to go see what the noise was. On the front of the closet, in what looked like blood, there was written, "God died here, you killed Him." I was scared. In my dream, I was naked and, as I tried to run back into the bedroom, a little man appeared. He said he was God and asked me why I was hiding from Him.

I told Him, "I don't know who you are."

And He said, "I am God. I made you. I died for you. I love you. Why do you ignore me?"

I was covering myself and trying to get back to bed—and He disappeared.

When I woke up, I was hyperventilating and shaking. I woke Fred and told him my dream. He was unconcerned. I told him I was going to go with his sister that night to the meeting. I immediately got up out of bed and phoned Sherry and said, "I am coming to the meeting tonight."

I told her my dream and she was thrilled. She was convinced that God was calling me. I am not one hundred percent sure it was directly from God, but it certainly got my attention. She had recently been converted and was very anxious to share her newfound joy. The fact that she wasn't drinking anymore seemed miraculous to me, so what did I have to lose?

I went to the meeting, and it was one of the strangest experiences I ever had. There were quite a few people there and the preacher was using a big screen with lots of animation. It was all new and very intriguing to me. I had never seen anything like it before. I went many other nights after and began feeling strange sensations. I was told these feelings were convictions and impressions. All I know is that I was falling in love with this Jesus, and He was way different from that version of Him I had met in Sunday school. This religion was complicated and had a lot of rules, but as is my nature, if I am going to go in, I am going to go all in. So, I did. I was baptized into this church.

The church said no alcohol or tobacco, so I immediately quit. The church said no caffeine or secular movies. I quit those too. My family and friends wondered what had happened to me. Had I joined a cult? I quit wearing makeup and pants. I stopped watching TV and listening to secular music. I became a vegetarian. If the church doors were open, I was there. I prayed. I read and studied my Bible. I witnessed and shared my faith. I went to almost every prayer meeting and camp meeting. I sang in church, taught Sabbath school, tithed, and eventually held evangelistic meetings myself.

If God had told me to give up anything at all, I would have done it. I was very close to God and rarely made a move or decision without praying for His will. I also wanted to convert my family and friends. My approach was not subtle and, although my family loved me very much, trying to convert them to my newfound religion and preach to them was not only ineffective, but extremely off-putting. I didn't see my mom and sister as much as I was used to when I was so heavily into church activities, but we were still close. I was quite one-dimensional and only able to discuss Jesus, salvation, or some other worship-related topic. I tried to get my mom and sister to come to church with me. I tried to share it with my dad. It seemed that all my efforts were in vain. I had little time for other interests because most all my activities revolved around the church. I may have mentioned that I tend to be an all-or-nothing kind of girl.

Attending church all the time, I made some good friends. It was great to have friends again. Fred was in and out of the church. For a period of time, he was all in and those were probably some of the happier times of our marriage.

After about a year in the church, I wanted a baby. Fred was not really interested in having children. I tried to convince him that we were in the family of God now and things would be different. I stopped taking birth control and he knew it. I got pregnant. I was super excited and felt sure he would be too, once he adjusted to the idea. I'm not sure if I subconsciously thought it would make our marriage better or if my maternal instinct was insatiable.

SELF-DENIAL WAS a major coping strategy for me and no matter how much I wished, wanted, or willed for a loving husband and healthy marriage, it just wasn't real. Fred was controlling and verbally abusive, even with his regular church attendance. The threat of physical violence was still always looming. He would get angry and slap or kick me. He spit on me, choked me, pushed me, and threw things at me. I did my best to keep him happy and avoid conflict. I walked on eggshells hoping to make the perfect house or be a good wife. Nothing pleased him. He was also obsessive about cleaning and militant about my participation. Looking back, I realize I was more of a slave than a wife. Although I worked full time, I was responsible for all of the house cleaning, laundry, cooking, and clean up.

One day when I was about six months pregnant, I was putting away some cassette tapes. I have no idea what set Fred off, but he came at me yelling and hit me in the head. I remember being so worried about my precious unborn child. As I crouched on the floor, after the unexpected attack, he came over and kicked me. The aim was my protruding belly, but I was able to blunt the force with my arms. Although I shouldn't have been surprised, I was. It was still somewhat shocking that he would stoop so low as to kick his pregnant wife. The day I delivered our daughter was the day after Thanksgiving. My mom came and stayed with me while I was in labor. I labored over eighteen hours but still had to have an emergency cesarean section. Fred was stoned as usual, but at least he showed up for the delivery. Later that month, I found out that, while I was recovering from the C-section birth of our daughter, he was at home running up credit card bills on phone sex.

Not long after Jennifer was born, Fred plunged into his crack cocaine addiction. He said he went to buy some marijuana and they offered him crack instead. It only took one or two times before he was hopelessly entangled. I would come home from work and notice items from our house missing. He was selling them for drugs. He burned through our savings and even began stealing. He'd become a full-blown addict. It was a horrific ordeal. He was not himself. His addiction made it even worse than before. It became obvious he could not stop on his own. I tried to get him some help, but you can't really help someone until they're ready. Of course, he blamed me for his addiction because, according to him, the reason he used was because he couldn't handle the stress of fatherhood. It was a common theme in our marriage: everything was always my fault.

I left. I took Jennifer and we stayed with some church friends. Fred was crazed and threatened to kill me and Jennifer. He said he was going to kill my mom and my whole family. I believed him. When he found out where we were staying, he threatened the family and, to my astonishment, the entire family packed up and moved. It was surreal. Jennifer and I moved in with another church family, but Fred was out of control. I honestly thought the only way to keep those I loved safe was to go back to him, so I did. What a nightmare!

I turned to the church in desperation, and they helped put him through one drug treatment center, and then another one. Even after all of that, when he got out of drug treatment, he convinced me to move away from my hometown, my family. He said it was the only way he could stay off drugs. I left everything I knew—my family, my friends, my job and my town. Jennifer was one year old and my mom was devastated. Another insane step in faith or blind commitment to this man. I quickly found a new church family and became immersed. Once again, I met friends and devoted so much of my life to the church. Jennifer was literally raised in the church. She had probably heard more sermons and evangelistic series by the time she was four than most people do in a lifetime. It was a great community and they helped me so much—I am forever grateful to them. Jennifer ended up choosing to go to a Christian boarding school. It was a great experience for her, with amazing opportunities, and it got her away from her dad. The church was also a haven for me. Even when my marriage was bad and things seemed intolerable, I had God, my ever-faithful source of comfort and peace.

Later in life, I would need to figure out how to separate my legalistic checklist religion and my true relationship with my God. I am not blaming my church family, but I will say they were adamantly opposed to divorce and made it clear God expected me to stay and support my husband. I can't really explain what exactly happened or why I left, but I believe it had something to do with feeling like I had to stay with Fred to remain in good standing with God. After ten years of devout and faithful service in the church, I just stopped going. The toxic relationship with Fred made me question my relationship with God. It was all so confusing and complicated, especially for Jennifer, who had grown up in church. She continued attending and praying for her parents. It was another difficult transition in our lives.

LOSING MY ROCK

*M*y mom was the second of five children. Her mother and father were loving parents who worked hard and always wanted the best for their children. My grandmother worked in the fields and then later took a full-time job with a florist, while also raising her children. The women in my family often boast that we came from a long line of strong women. My mom was easygoing and had a real zest for life. She married my dad, even though my grandparents didn't really approve. They said he was from the wrong side of the tracks, but she was so in love. My dad was a bit of a rambling soul, with frequent job changes and the desire to move to different towns. It was true that he was from a different socioeconomic class. His parents died young, his brothers were both alcoholics, and he basically fended for himself from a very young age. Despite his upbringing, he loved my mom and was a decent provider. They were married for seventeen years, and when my dad left, he broke my mother's heart. She was never really the same. Although mom eventually went on with her life, even remarrying, she loved my father until her dying day.

My grandma had my mom when she was twenty-three years old, and my mom had me when she was twenty-three, and I had Jennifer when I was twenty-three. Jennifer wisely broke that tradition. She chose to finish college before starting a family. Our family is small but very tight knit. My mom and I were super close and, although she loved her mom, she was definitely closer to her daddy. When my grandpa died, it left a huge hole in my mom's heart, and she always believed that Jennifer was born to help heal that hole.

To say that Jennifer was the highlight of my mom's life is hardly an overstatement. Mom loved Jennifer as much —or maybe even more than—she loved me. Perhaps this is nothing to write home about and all mother–daughter–granddaughter relationships are like this. I don't know. What I do know is that through everything that has happened in my life, my mom was there for me. When Fred became abusive, she was there begging me to leave. When I chose to stay in a bad marriage, she was still there for me. When my baby was born, my mom was there with me the entire time. When I went to nursing school, I swear she was as anxious and nervous about every single test grade as I was, always believing in me and so very proud. I could call my mom and talk with her for hours about anything or nothing. When I graduated nursing school, she was there at the pinning, beaming with pride. Every event in my life, good or bad, my mom was there for me. I never gave a thought to there being a day she wouldn't be there anymore.

It was February 1999. My daughter was thirteen years

old. She was becoming a typical teenager, but way better than I ever was. She spent a lot of time with my mom, even though we lived a state away. Jennifer spent several weeks in the summer at my mom's and took many road trips with her and her new husband. She loved being at grandma's house, probably because she got away from the stress of her own home. Of course, all the special attention and spoiling she received could have been a contributing factor. My mom had more pictures of Jennifer on her walls than there was room for. Despite our physical distance, there was probably not ever a time when I went more than six weeks or so without seeing my mom. Did I mention we were close?

My mom began complaining about some chest pain. She went to the doctor and was told it was costochondritis (inflammation of the breastbone). Mom had an HMO insurance policy, so with each visit she had to go back to her primary care physician to get approval for additional tests or visits with the specialist. The PCP, however, is incentivized to keep costs down by not ordering expensive tests or making referrals to a specialist. This physician continued to change the diagnosis (without ordering a CT scan or MRI) from costochondritis, to gallbladder issues, to bile duct obstruction, and finally to diabetes before mom ended up in the emergency room with severe pain. The ER physician ordered a CT scan and saw the large mass on the head of her pancreas. I was furious that she had endured months of misdiagnoses and unnecessary treatments, but realistically an earlier diagnosis likely would not have improved the outcome.

I remember the week before her biopsy results came in I drove down to spend the weekend with her. Jennifer was playing with the neighbor kids. My mom and I laid on her bed and discussed the what if. What if it is cancer? Neither of us wanted to think this could be possible. We cried a little but mostly stayed in the moment of us just holding hands, talking, and being together. I remember going out to dinner and laughing. I remember the hugs and I love yous. I remember the tears when we got ready to go home Sunday afternoon.

It seemed like a long time since the weekend, but it was probably only Thursday. I was working for a physician in a small office as his nurse and office manager. I loved that job. Still to this day it was one of my favorite positions. My coworker and longtime friend Missy took the call. I was with a patient. Missy came back and said, "Your mom is on the phone."

My heart stopped. It was before cell phones and my mom never called me at work. I picked up the phone with my heart racing. "Mom, is everything okay?"

"I have cancer," she said with a brave but tearful voice.

I said, "What kind? Do they know?"

She said, "Pancreatic."

I don't remember the rest of the conversation or even the rest of that day. I was in shock. As a nurse, I knew pancreatic cancer was likely a death sentence.

I am very thankful that I was not drinking during this time. My mom's death was during my ten-year religious journey. Being strong in my faith saved me and was a wonderful comfort to my mom. I shudder to imagine what would have happened if I had been using alcohol. I saw what happened to my sister CC, her world spinning out of control, alcohol fueling even more depression and anxiety. All I could do was pray.

The next ten months were some of the most precious and painful. I visited my mom almost every other weekend and had her come and visit me. I was there for as many doctor visits as I could be. When I couldn't be there, I would call the office and ask the physician to call me. The prognosis was not good. The surgeon would attempt the Whipple procedure, which only had a fifty percent survival rate, and, even if successful, the aftermath would not be promising. The day my mom went to surgery was extremely scary. Best case scenario, she would wake up in the ICU having endured a successful surgery with a twenty-five percent chance of surviving five years. Worst case, she would wake up in a regular hospital bed expecting an expiration date of three to six months. I said my tearful goodbye at her bedside and waited for the outcome. I remember when she woke up from anesthesia, she looked around the room and said, "I am going to die."

Mom was a sharp cookie and quickly realized she was in a regular room surrounded by her family. She began to sob. This was one of the few times I saw her cry for herself. The only other times she really cried about her looming death was when she talked about not being able to see Jennifer grow up.

How do you say goodbye to a part of your heart? The mother-child bond is indescribably powerful. It has to be one of the most important and critical relationships we ever have. I realize many people are not as fortunate as I was. Not all mothers are loving and nurturing. Let's face it, my mom was no saint, but her love for me was unconditional. It was an intense, unselfish, pure love that I will never experience again from anyone. She didn't want to leave me or her loved ones, but she accepted her fate without complaining. I'm not sure that I would handle a death sentence as gracefully as she did. Knowing you have an expiration date (as my sister later said) changes everything. Immediately, material goods lose their value. Money takes a backseat and any striving or attempts at increasing the ego are fruitless. Life becomes so very precious. Spending time with loved ones, enjoying simple pleasures and being connected to your spirituality are really the only things that matter. Mom made the most of her last days. We have a ton of stories and experiences during her last ten months. Obviously, a big goal was keeping her as healthy and as pain-free as possible for her remaining days.

The hospice nurse who was present at my mom's death said something that I would not understand for many years. My mom was surrounded by her loved ones and we were singing hymns. I told her to go. She had fought a good fight and I promised her I would be okay. She took her last breath, then I dissolved into tears and began sobbing uncontrollably. The hospice nurse was crying too, and she simply said, "That was a beautiful death."

A beautiful death? I didn't know how much those words would mean to me later on. It was indeed a beautiful death. Being surrounded by your loved ones with no regrets or unresolved issues, having a trusting faith in God—what more could any of us ask for?

DEATH IS the one thing we all share. Every person, rich or poor, healthy or sick, will eventually die.

My mom's death rocked my world and shook me to

the core. I believe my sister's suffering was even worse than mine. She may have had regrets, or it may have been she still saw herself as a child that needed her mommy. I don't know. But it was a dark time for all of us. I cried for months. I didn't know how I could go on. I worked and did my best to take care of Jennifer, but my grief was unbearable. Jennifer was devastated too, our lives altered forever. I could no longer trust the future. I struggled with balancing living for the moment and planning for the future. It was then, and always will be, the cruelest lesson in the fragility of life. My mom had plans to retire and move up near me; that never happened. She was going to do so many things but never got the chance. It was life-altering for me, and I began to accept that no one is promised tomorrow. At age fifty-nine, my mom was gone and I would be forced to navigate the world without her.

"Grief is the price we pay for love."

— -QUEEN ELIZABETH II

THIS WAS the beginning of my journey to myself. From that day forward, I would have an aching in my soul that would push me to pursue my dreams and live my best life. I made my final failed attempt at leaving Fred less than a year after my mom's death. Status quo was no longer an option.

DRINKING AT WORK

*O*ver the course of my career as I moved into different healthcare management roles, I was sometimes afforded the opportunity to go out of town for conferences or seminars. Being on my own, if only for a couple nights, was always extremely welcome and exciting. I would inevitably end up closing down the bars with fellow attendees or employees from the vendor companies. A couple of times, I barely made it back to my room before sunrise.

One of my favorite events was held in Boston. It was a user conference. The electronic medical records company my practice used had sponsored an annual user conference for people to network, learn more efficient ways to use their product, and share feedback about potential enhancements. The classes during the day were very informative and it was great to have access to the creators of the software system to share our frustrations and concerns. It was also a good way to meet people from all over that could share their workarounds and best practices. The company was wise to hold these events and, man, did they know how to throw a party! If the goal was to get their clients to want to come back the following year, they were successful. There was great food, the hotel was fabulous, and the after-hours entertainment was the best. One year they hired a comedian, the next year they did a disco party, and the following year the event had a casino theme. The open bar started serving immediately after classes and kept going way into the night. Free booze made it easy to keep the party going and I was notorious for being the life of the party.

Every year my reputation preceded me, and I was quickly surrounded by fellow partiers who knew we would be finding the afterparty. My second year at this event was when they hosted the disco party. Everyone was all dressed up in seventies attire and boogieing down. You can picture me in a brown afro wig with psychedelic bell bottoms, platform shoes, a cute tank top, and a large peace sign necklace. I had bright blue eye shadow, retro red loop earrings, and I was feeling good. When we finished up the scheduled party around 11 p.m., a group of us headed down the street to another bar. There were probably fifteen or twenty of us there and someone else was picking up the booze tab, though I didn't know who.

Next thing I knew, that bar was closing because it was now 2 a.m. As we made our way out into the cool night air, I asked, "Is that it? Do we have to go back to the hotel now?"

Somebody in the group said, "Hell no," and hailed a cab.

It was a smaller group by now, maybe only eight or ten of us, as we piled into taxis headed who knows where. We end up at this restaurant—I would say it was Chinese, but I couldn't be sure—and the local Bostonian leading the group ordered some kind of special "tea." I took a sip of mine when it arrived. Lo and behold, more alcohol—the teapot was filled with beer. We sat around the table drinking our "tea" and eating food until 4 a.m. It was the craziest thing I had ever seen.

The next morning, I missed the first few classes. I think a few of us did. When I finally made it down for the coffee and carbs, I saw some of the others, all of us looking like crap, dehydrated and hungover, but bragging about our escapade and counting the minutes until cocktail hour when we could get a little "hair of the dog." My nickname after that event was "catalyst." I got the credit—or the blame—for fueling the all-night drinking frenzy.

On another trip away from home, I was the speaker. I was doing a series of seminars as a side hustle. When the seminar was over, of course I headed to the bar. After all, eating alone is best at the bar with other folks who're by themselves, right? I met some new friends and we stayed up drinking half the night. Looking back, it is quite amazing that nothing bad ever happened to me during these trips. It is probably even more unbelievable that I never cheated on Fred. It was just fun to be free for a few nights, and alcohol helped me reduce my inhibitions. Unfortunately, the next day's seminar was at 8 a.m., and I was likely still partially intoxicated and absolutely hungover. My eyes were bloodshot and I felt awful. I was sucking down Tylenol and Gatorade and pretty sure everyone in the audience knew I had overindulged the night before. I have no idea how I made it through the class, but I vowed not to do that again, at least not when I was the one doing the presentation.

My alcohol use after the ten-year teetotaling period, but before I left Fred, was moderate. I would binge drink when I was out of the house and away from Fred, which rarely happened, but when I was at home, I never felt safe enough to lose myself in alcohol. Drinking too much when I was with Fred was too dangerous; I probably didn't trust myself, fearing I might say something I shouldn't say. After I left Fred, though, I drank almost every day.

As I climbed the corporate ladder, drinking was not only welcome but expected. I attended a lot of physician recruitment dinners and business meetings. As the dinner or meeting would start, the physicians and executives clamored to share their fine taste and knowledge of wine. Being a red wine lover, these dinners were always a great treat, as I got to taste and experience very expensive wines that I otherwise would never have been able to afford. Dinner tabs with only six or seven guests added up to thousands of dollars. Wine flowed without economic concern and the waitstaff made sure the glasses were never empty. You had to be quite diligent not to get sloppy drunk at these events. I was experiencing a taste of how the other half lived and I liked it. Learning about the flavors and notes of high-dollar wines, being taught how to swirl and smell and sip, I was becoming quite fluent in the art of classy drinking. It was so much more acceptable and posher to be drinking a three-hundred-fifty-dollar bottle of wine than some MD 20/20 or a six pack of Natural Lite. The rich food and expensive wine were part of the deal. Out of all the dinners and meetings I have attended over the years, there were very few people, physicians or otherwise, who didn't drink. Being on call was really the only acceptable excuse, after all—no one wants their heart surgeon having a few drinks before getting called in to do their life-saving, open-heart surgery.

Entertaining potential new physician partners and their spouses always involved a nice, relaxed dinner, with alcohol flowing. I remember one group of physicians I worked with who were really big drinkers. One insisted on some special imported rum that he wanted me to try, and the other physicians were wine connoisseurs. There were several late nights drinking with this group, even after the physician candidate was long gone. For one particular recruitment dinner, reservations were made at a very nice restaurant about twenty minutes from my house. The wine was flowing and the visiting physician was a lot of fun. We also had a consultant in the office for the day, Deb, who came to the dinner. These dinners could last for hours, everyone talking and taking through the appetizers, main course, and then dessert. It was probably close to 9:30 when I was ready to leave. I knew I was too drunk to drive home.

I commented to one of the physicians, "I am kind of worried about driving home."

Instead of getting me a cab or insisting I make other arrangements home, he said, "If you get pulled over, call me."

He had some pull with police and could help me out if necessary. I made it home that night without any issues, but when I woke up in the morning, I couldn't find my phone. I searched my car then thought I might have left it at the restaurant. I was living with Andy (you'll meet him later), but he was out of town for work, so I showered, got dressed, and drove into the office.

I saw Deb in the hall and told her I had lost my phone. She said, "It has to be in your car or at your house. Don't you remember? I talked to you on your way home last night."

I said, "Oh yeah, that's right. I forgot."

But the truth was that I had absolutely no recollection of talking to her. I was mortified. I drove back home and found my cell phone, dead, laying on the floor under my bed. How many times had I driven home when I shouldn't have? I was usually very careful to make plans or simply not drive, but truthfully even one time is too many. I shudder to think what could have happened. My life or someone else's taken or ruined in a flash because of a stupid decision.

If you have ever been to a work function or event where alcohol was served, you know that there is always someone who has a little too much to drink and ends up being the talk of the office the next day. I've definitely been that person a time or two. Usually, if you are the poor drunk, you often don't remember exactly what happened and your coworkers or employees likely won't talk to you about what happened. They talk about you to others. I can recount so many Christmas parties, company picnics, and other events where people had to be poured into a taxi or driven home. There was one after-work mixer planned at a nearby Mexican restaurant during which the company was offering free wine, beer and appetizers, and it was all going smoothly until one of the physician leaders showed up and started buying shots of tequila. Some outlandish behavior followed, including some dirty dancing and a couple of minor injuries. I believe someone in the risk department showed up and started offering free hotel rooms and insisting on cab rides home. That was the last alcoholic mixer we had while I worked there.

What is especially interesting about work drinking and alcohol-fueled after work fun is that you see the smart, responsible, respectable people you work with every day in a completely different way. Alcohol does reduce your inhibitions and people under the influence do or say things they would never do or say sober. I was always a big fan of alcohol at work functions and, as a leader myself, very often promoted and planned events with lots of drinking, but if I'm honest, some of the things I saw people say or do under the influence changed the way I saw them forever. Seeing your highly acclaimed surgeon, slugging down vodka, slurring his words, and flirting with the young female employees can be unsettling. It is often those of us with high-pressure, stressful roles, that find the most comfort and relief in alcohol.

I have only had to endure a few company dinner parties after I quit drinking. Unfortunately, they are much different when you don't indulge. One of the first dinners I attended sober was kind of an intimate group. There were only six of us: three physicians, the physician recruiter, the CEO, and me. The usual conversation about wine began—who preferred white or red—and an impressive list of everyone's favorites. An expensive red wine was chosen. I cringed. It would be my first real temptation sober. I quickly told the group I was on an alcohol-free challenge and would not be drinking. The usual whys were batted around and, once convinced I would indeed not be drinking that night, they carried on without me. I could smell the vino as the waitress poured it. I watched one of the physicians do the obligatory swirl and sip, approving the bottle of wine. Then came the descriptions of the flavor: hickory notes with just the right amount of dryness. I have to admit that my mouth was watering and my senses were on high alert. It had been less than thirty days since I had had a drink, and it took a bit of white knuckling to turn it down. Once the second bottle was uncorked, I began to see the changes in my dinner companions. They were getting a little louder and less articulate, no one sloppy drunk yet, but the conversation was going downhill fast. One physician was repeating his point *ad nauseam* and another one was attempting to talk over him. Teeth were turning purple and eyes became a bit glassy. I saw how the wine was changing them. I was not envious anymore; I was ready to go and, before dessert was served, excused myself and made a quiet exit. Driving home sober, I felt proud of myself. I had made it through my first drinking dinner with my alcohol of choice flowing and my glass filled with water. This was definitely a new experience for me. I was seeing, maybe for the first time ever, what alcohol looks like to the sober observer—and it was not flattering.

THE NEXT CHAPTER

*T*he first year of freedom, if I'm being honest, was a real period of exploration. Time to discover myself and surround myself with family and friends. I even had a best friend, Lexie. She was there for me when I left Fred and we have been through a lot together since then. She is more like family to me now. I met Lexie a few years earlier. She worked for me and was one of my very best managers. She enjoys data, details, and spreadsheets—exactly who a "big picture" visionary person like myself needs to be successful and get shit done. Lexi undervalued herself, as many of us do. She lived in a small town and worked in a local company with little aspiration for advancement. That is one of the many things I love about Lexie: she is rock steady and content, so the polar opposite of me. Lexie is a few years younger too. She was married for a brief period and now proclaims, "When I am tired of being happy, I will look for my next ex-husband." She keeps her hair cut short, stands probably five inches taller than me, and has a few extra pounds in tow. I would not consider her a girly girl. She doesn't wear makeup, jewelry, or care about the latest fashion, but she carries herself well and is beautiful in her own right. Lexie is an introvert and hates being the center of attention. It is rare for her to voluntarily share her feelings or start a conversation about herself. She has a heart of gold and is the most dependable person I know. If Lexie says she is going to do it, consider it done, at work or otherwise. I immediately liked her from the first day I met her. She was funny and kind—and way smarter than she'd give herself credit for. When I left the company, I asked her if we could still be friends, and she said "sure," but later confessed that she didn't even know we were friends and never for one minute believed I would call or keep in touch.

Within a few months, I recruited Lexie to join my new organization. Over the years, we have worked together many times. The dynamic duo, with me out front and her the detailed brains behind the operation. She hates public speaking, leading meetings, and being in the spotlight, and I hate spreadsheets! After I left Fred, Lexie and I spent a ton of time together. She is a great listener and always answered my late-night drunk calls. It wasn't even a month after my escape when Lexie found out she had breast cancer. We were quite the pair. We would try to take care of each other. It was probably a good distraction for us both. I was in a great deal of emotional pain and turmoil with the divorce, and she was dealing with the emotional and physical trauma of her cancer diagnosis. I remember one day we were at my apartment, as we often were. I heated up a small frozen pizza and we split it. Neither of us wanted to eat, both of us trying to make sure the other got some kind of nutrition. I bet we nibbled on that cardboard pizza for more than an hour. Those were some really rough times, dealing with the drama and antics of my ex, her surgery and chemotherapy, and coping with our new realities, but these deeply felt experiences bonded us like we had been friends for a hundred years.

During this time, I drank too much, partied like I was in college, and did whatever the hell I wanted. I was working my ass off at work and enjoying my newfound freedom. Yes, I was grieving and trying to find out how to function in my new single status, but I also began to feel a sense of relief. I didn't have to walk on eggshells anymore. It was scary being on my own, but it was also peaceful. I no longer lived in dread or fear, except for what he might do next.

I began slowly working on purchases to restart my life. I had to purchase every pot, pan, and towel. I started buying lamps, furniture, and art that I liked. It was truly like starting over. I was driving a blue Chevy Impala with over three hundred fifty thousand miles on it. It had been in a few fender benders and looked pretty rough. The car was in the shop every other day for repairs, but the final straw was getting into an accident, which pulled off the rear bumper. I had friends help me shove the bumper in the back seat of the car.

Chuck, my boss, said, "Janet, please get another car. Don't keep driving that thing here."

I guess it was embarrassing to see the COO of the company pulling in with that trashed up beater. I knew I had to get another car. Lexie went with me to look at cars. We parked down the road so no one could see what I was driving. We didn't want anyone to know how desperately I needed a new ride. After a great deal of online searching and a couple of visits to car dealerships, I decided on an affordable Chrysler convertible. Yes, a convertible was just what I needed. I drove my Impala, overheating and with the bumper in the back seat, to the local dealership to make the trade. I wrote a check for eleven thousand dollars and went into the bathroom to throw up. My first independent big purchase in years, maybe ever. I was certain the car was going to be unreliable and that I had made a mistake. When you have been belittled and treated like you are stupid for so long, you question every decision. To this day, part of my daily affirmation is, "I make smart decisions." You would not believe the hours of therapy, self-development work and books read to get those negative tapes out of my head. Well, I loved my convertible and it turned out to be a really good car. I remember driving home from work with the top down, heading to my sparsely furnished, little, one-bedroom apartment. I had to drive right past the Wrigley's production facility. The sweet aroma of the Juicy Fruit they were making brought a smile to my face. The smell of Juicy Fruit will forever in my mind be a sweet reminder of joyous freedom!

I started making friends and meeting people. I have always been a very social person and now I had the opportunity to pursue it. I even dated a nice guy for a while. His name was John. He was kindhearted, and the way he tolerated and dealt with my post-traumatic stress was genuinely a gift. He was the exact opposite of my ex. John was nice, loving, and treated me like a queen. It was the perfect rebound relationship, and I will always have a special place in my heart for this man who helped me through such a trying time. We had a lot of fun together and did a bunch of cool things, but we were in different places in our lives, and it had to end.

I moved four times in less than two years. Apartment living was tough for me. Leaving the house I'd built and paid for was painful. I missed the garage. I missed my yard. I missed having all my stuff. A friend of mine was trying to sell his house and offered to let me live there for what I was paying for my apartment. He had moved away and his house was sitting empty. Lucky for me, the house was a mansion, or at least it was to me. It was massive, with six bedrooms and six bathrooms, a huge kitchen, a two-car garage, a wrap-around deck, a formal living room, a den, and a basement. The house was practically empty. I didn't have enough furniture to fill up my little apartment, so this giant house really looked bare. My daughter moved in with me—there was plenty of room for her. We would have friends over and everyone could spend the night. Lexie had a room there, and even though she didn't really live with us, she was there as much as I was.

We celebrated Christmas in that amazing house that year. I bought a huge Christmas tree to fill the space. I surrounded myself with friends and family. Aunt J and her hubby were there, my sister CC came, and so did Jennifer and her faithful pup Freckman, Lexie, and John and his kids too. It was wonderful. That Christmas there was no fear of anyone throwing Christmas presents out the front door and ruining the day—no temper tantrums, no dismay. My mother-in-law even spent Christmas with us, as she did many years. She and I had always been close and, honestly, she knew exactly what I had dealt with all these years. While she loved her son, she didn't excuse his bad behavior and had made the difficult decision to sever ties with him as well for her own self-preservation. I was not the only one Fred lashed out at. It was a happy time with lots of presents, food, and laughter. I also had a New Year's Eve party. The house was packed. I was having the time of my life.

I had a lot of fun playing house in my friend's pad, but I didn't get to stay there long. The realtors said my "lawn furniture" set up in the house was making it hard to show and sell. Yes, I had a patio table in the dining room, but it was all I could afford. Anyway, my friend asked me to move so he could sell his house. It was fun while it lasted. I ended up getting a rental house that Jennifer and I moved into. She lived with me until she finished college and moved out.

There were a ton of adventures during that first few years. Lexie and I visited my dad in Florida several times. He and Bertha played in a band. They played gigs at places like the Moose Lodge, VFW clubs, and dive bars. Dad would invite me up to sing a song or two. We hung out with the old folk "groupies" and getting drunk was always super inexpensive at these venues. Lots of good times, but lots of drinking too.

This was also the year Lexie and I were invited to our first Girls' Weekend with ToriJill and Sophie, a couple of ladies we knew from work. The four of us are still close. We get together every year for our annual Girls' Weekend. We even took a trip to Italy together one year. Another year we ventured up to Maine, Boston, and New Hampshire. During our first weekend together at ToriJill's lake house, we shared some of our intimate secrets. We laughed, we cried, and we cemented our friendships. I am so fortunate to have them in my life. Friendships like ours are very hard to find.

Another exciting thing I tried was online dating. I signed up for eHarmony, but it was too slow and controlled for me. I found a free dating website called Plenty of Fish and decided to check it out. I went out with a couple of guys but no one that I really liked. I enjoyed the attention, the chats, and the banter. If I met a guy and wasn't interested, I ended it quickly and moved forward. One evening, I was checking out my site hits and this guy popped up. He was cute and had a wacky profile. It said something like he wasn't interested in dating if you had a profile picture of your cat or dog and not to bother contacting him if you had tattoos, fake boobs, or collagen lips. He talked about loving Cheap Trick and being open to adventure. His closing line said something hilarious like he might still be interested if you didn't meet these criteria but had a great set of tits. It was by far the most unique profile I'd read and it made me laugh. I'm sure I was close to the bottom of my bottle of merlot when I responded. My reply was "they are real and they are spectacular," a quote from *Seinfeld*. I guess that caught his attention, so we started chatting. We spent a few nights chatting back and forth on Plenty of Fish and then he asked for my phone number. After a few relatively normal phone calls, we decided to meet in person for a date.

His name was Andy. At fifty-four years old, he'd just barely made my age cutoff of eight years older than me. He had a good stable job and seemed like a stand-up guy. I liked that he was witty and funny, and he was easy to talk to. Dating at this stage in life was a different animal. Basically, you pretty much have to figure out what kind of baggage the person has and if you can tolerate it, then find out how willing the other person is to accept your baggage, because at our age we all have baggage. I remember watching this silly show one time called *Baggage*. It was a very funny show, kind of like *The Dating Game*. In one episode, a female contestant met three male contestants who told her a little bit about themselves and why she should choose to date them, but then a "piece of baggage" was revealed about each man. The lady had to decide which baggage she couldn't live with and eliminate that guy. Of course, the baggage on the show was usually something super shocking or outrageous. My baggage, a psycho ex-husband, PTSD from his abuse, and much more. What about Andy? What were the skeletons in his closet? He had two sons, one nine and the other seventeen. They lived with their mother, but they stayed with him a lot. He lived not too far from his children. I thought that might be a deal breaker. I love kids, but my daughter was grown and heading off on her own. I was in a selfish stage of discovery and freedom. I was not even remotely thinking about family or kids. Turns out those boys would become a wonderful addition to my life and family.

Our infamous first date is something worth sharing. We met at a trendy restaurant nearby. I remember when I first saw him that I was immediately drawn to his striking blue eyes. He was wearing a tweed jacket and jeans. He was very attractive. Gray hair, medium build, and a beautiful smile. It was easy conversation as we shared a bottle of wine. We talked about our recent dating experiences, family, previous marriages, jobs, sports, and more. After we finished a delicious dinner and polished off a second bottle of wine, we left the restaurant. When we got outside, the night was young. I guess neither of us really wanted the date to end. We talked about going somewhere else and maybe having another drink. The only place we could think of nearby was a redneck karaoke bar down the road. I got in his car and we traveled to the local dive. Music was blaring and lots of people were dancing. We had a beer or two and continued to talk. I was feeling the alcohol by then for sure. I was dancing, which is certainly the norm for me. He still teases me about our first-date booty grind. It was my signature move, after having way too much booze. Who could resist that? Ha! We stayed awhile longer then decided to go and grab a bite at Waffle House. From a fancy restaurant to a redneck bar and then to Waffle House—that had to be the perfect date, right? The night was far from over. We got to experience a real-life girl fight (actual jumping up on the table) and a drunk almost peeing on Andy's feet in the men's bathroom. Oh, what a night! One of things I really love about Andy is that he's comfortable in any setting. We can go to a dive or a five-star restaurant. Maybe it is his salesman background, but Andy can talk and fit in with almost any crowd.

Andy called me the next day and we made plans to go out again the following weekend. He knew a guy in a band, and they were playing in a town not too far away. He picked me up and we ended up in yet another seedy dump. The band was good and we enjoyed the vibe, but someone—probably me—thought it would be a good idea to do some shots. The next thing we knew, we were doing shots with this crazy couple we'd just met, Ester and

Melvin. Apparently it was Melvin's birthday. At one point, Melvin or Ester suggested we spend the night with them across the street at their hotel. I obviously didn't know Andy very well, but I told him in no uncertain terms that if we ended up with that couple, I was going with Ester. Of course, I was joking—there was no way I was going anywhere with them. We ended up driving home that night in the pouring rain. Probably not our best decision, but thankfully we survived. Date two in the books, another rousing adventure.

Andy was somewhat aloof and a bit of a loner. He would call me every few days or so. Since he traveled for work, we would make plans to see each other maybe one evening a week and most weekends. I don't think it had been all that long when we had our "fishing pole" talk.

We were out to dinner, and Andy asked, "What would you think about being my girlfriend and taking our fishing poles out of the Plenty of Fish pond?" He always had a way of making me laugh which was one of the many things I liked about him, but this conversation was serious.

I said, "What would be the benefit of being your girl-friend?" He rattled off an impressive list, so I agreed. We began dating exclusively and removed our profiles from the dating sites. It wasn't difficult for me—being in a monogamous relationship was my comfort zone. Having someone care about me but not smother me or need to know my every action was a new experience for me. Andy was perfect! I went out with girlfriends, made trips to see family, and carried on with my life. He was a stable guy, settled in his career, and he enjoyed spending time with his sons. If we got together, great! But if we didn't, there was no twenty questions or hell to pay. At first, I couldn't decide if he was secure in our relationship or just didn't give a shit. It took me over a year to realize that he just wasn't the jealous type. He was only married for a few years and, while being a father was his proudest achievement, being a husband was not so much. Our casual yet committed relationship worked for us.

Andy and I settled into a wonderful routine. He's smart and fun, and I really enjoyed our time together. He played the guitar and we spent a lot of time drinking, singing, and laughing. I got to know his boys, Paul and Felix. At seventeen, Paul was busy with his career preparation, social life, and friends. I didn't see him a lot, but Felix was only nine and he was with us all the time. Felix and I quickly became buddies. I had never been around little boys, but it sure was fun. I was grateful Andy had sons. I turned them on to my "wicked awesome" dessert, and that was enough for them to accept me. Our blended family was taking shape. I adored Andy's mom. Andy tolerated my dad and I think their love of music helped with that bond. We spent a lot of time on The Settlement; that's what I named the boat, since it was one of the only things I got out of the divorce. Boating on the lake was great fun. Andy is a skilled captain and everyone loved going out. I'd had no idea what a relaxing day of boating was like—it was incredible. There were so many things I'd done in the past that I thought were stressful or challenging, but I found it depends on who you do them with. Felix was available to go with us the most, but Paul and Jennifer joined us as often as they could.

I bought my first house and was enjoying the freedom to paint, decorate, and furnish it the way I wanted to. For the first time in my life, I got to decide what color to paint the walls and what kind of furniture to buy. I have to admit any major decisions sent me into a tailspin. I struggle, to this day, with trusting my decisions, but I am so much better now. Even as time has proven I make smart choices, the fear can be paralyzing. Andy and Jennifer were a big help with the house purchase. We must have looked at fifty houses before deciding on the one to buy. All of this independence was uncharted territory, but I loved it. I was also busy trying to complete my education. Working full time, having a great social life, exploring who and what I liked, and working on my master's degree —well, you know what they say—if you want something done, give it to a busy person.

At some point, I began feeling the love bug. I was falling in love with Andy, but I wasn't sure the feeling was mutual. It wasn't easy to tell with Andy, plus I didn't have all that much experience with romantic love. We talked, we shared, and we kissed—a lot and everywhere we went. I was relieved he was not opposed to public displays of affection. Boy, that seems like a lifetime ago. Anyway, knowing his fear of commitment and his loner mentality, I was afraid a discussion about love and our future together would push him away. I recall the cryptic conversation well. We were on the phone and, of course, I went for it. I asked about whether we were in the same book, if we were in the same chapter or even on the same page.

I asked, "Are we reading the same book of love and commitment? It's okay if I'm a few chapters ahead, but if you're not even reading the same book and don't have any interest in reading it at all, then I probably need to cut my losses before I invest more of my heart."

He said, "I am reading the book and I'm just about to turn the page to the chapter you're on."

What a relief. I kind of thought we were both feeling it, but I'd been wrong before. We were in different stages of our lives, with different histories, but neither of us wanted to play games or pretend. We were mature enough at that time in our lives to be who we were. Both of us were looking for someone to accept us as we are without lies, pretense, or unrealistic expectations. For me, being liked and loved for who I am was all I wanted. Both of us are jaded by our pasts in our own ways, neither of us wanting to get married or expecting someone else to take care of us or fix us. This relationship was easy. I didn't have to walk on eggshells or try to make him happy by changing who I was.

Not long after we started dating, he'd jokingly said, "I should thank your ex-husband since he set the bar so low. It's easy to make you happy."

He still, to this day, says that his number one job is to make me happy. Now I realize no one else can make you happy, but it is certainly nice to be with someone willing to try. In many ways, he is right that my relationship expectations were probably pretty low, but to give him due credit, he is a very thoughtful, mature, and caring man that gives me the space to be me and truly accepts me, flaws and all.

If you would have told me that Andy and I would get married one day, I would have bet you large sums of money that that would never happen. Never say never.

CANCER

My life was going great. I was enjoying my first home independently and was in a wonderful relationship with Andy, a man who wasn't needy. I had developed tons of friendships, my daughter was heading off to complete her graduate degree, and I was close to finishing my master's degree. I had overcome the horrible divorce and was soaking up all the goodness of my new life. It felt like I had been given a second chance for happiness and I was taking it. Boating, hiking, and all sorts of new adventures and experiences. Life was good.

I was healthy. I only went to the doctor once a year and that was to the gynecologist for my annual pap. I worked in healthcare, so most of my illnesses or ailments were treated with hallway consults. It was February when I went for my annual gynecology visit. I saw the nurse practitioner who did the routine breast exam, inquired about my mammogram, and performed the dreaded pap smear. She asked if I was having any other issues, and I

75

only briefly mentioned that I had been experiencing a good deal of constipation and a bit of itching/anal pain lately. To her credit, she decided to do a rectal exam. After the exam she reassured me that I had hemorrhoids and gave me a prescription for an extra-strength hemorrhoid cream.

For the next year, I largely ignored any further symptoms, since I had been confidently diagnosed with hemorrhoids. I used the cream and other comfort measures throughout the year. By January of the following year, my symptoms had gotten way worse. I was even noticing a little blood now and then with my bowel movements. This was all "normal" for someone with internal hemorrhoids, according to Dr. Google. Discussing the anus, bowel movements and hemorrhoids is not something most of us embrace. It is somewhat embarrassing to talk about being constipated or having an itchy butt.

The following February rolled around, and it was time once again for my annual female visit. I got the call that my appointment was slated for the next day or two, but before my appointment I received another phone call saying my physician was going to be out of town and that my visit had been changed to seeing the nurse practitioner. I was fine with that—no problem. This visit was again routine with basically no changes in my gynecological status. The breast exam and the pap smear test are necessary evils most women are well acquainted with. This year I complained a little more vehemently about my bowel situation. The constipation had greatly increased, I was uncomfortable a lot of the time, and I even mentioned the blood I had seen. She didn't seem alarmed since I had internal hemorrhoids and all of those symptoms were expected. Once again, she did her due diligence with a rectal exam. It was extremely uncomfortable this time. She said my hemorrhoids were huge and that I really needed to add more fiber in my diet. She gave me a pamphlet on how to care for hemorrhoids, two types of cream, and samples of Metamucil. I was reassured that a lot of people suffer from hemorrhoids, and indeed all the symptoms were familiar and clearly documented. I just needed to be more diligent with the fiber in my diet and use the prescriptions faithfully.

One morning in early April, I woke up with a horrible sensation. It felt as if something had fallen into my vagina. Being a nurse, I feared that I had a rectocele or cystocele —that my rectum or bladder had prolapsed or fallen into my vagina. I was already dreading the bladder tack—a procedure I would likely need. I even began thinking about the mesh or no-mesh alternatives involved in the procedure when I placed the call to my gynecology office. Once again, the physician was not available and it was the same nurse practitioner who would be able to see me that day. I often wonder whether, if my physician had seen me instead of the nurse practitioner on just one of these visits, the outcome would have been different. This time, my visit was totally focused on whatever was causing the pushing, full sensation in my vaginal area. Was it a huge out-of-control hemorrhoid that had finally gotten so big it was pushing through my vaginal wall? She examined me and declared I was full of shit—literally. She said that I had so much stool in my rectum it was pushing into my vaginal wall and that I had to increase my fiber intake or even take laxatives if needed. I left unconvinced. I did some research and then asked a friend working in the field to recommend a reputable colorectal physician. I decided I might either have the world's biggest hemorrhoid or be full of shit, but something was going to have to give. Thankfully, my insurance company allowed self-referrals and I reluctantly called to schedule my appointment with the recommended colorectal surgeon.

It was May tenth, when I arrived for my appointment filled with dread. I felt embarrassed and was sure I was wasting the physician's time. I remember in our initial conversation me telling him about my symptoms, previous diagnosis, and basically apologizing for being there wasting his time. He was a wonderful physician, very caring and kind. He assured me that I was in the right place and that there were lots of very effective treatments for hemorrhoids, if that was what it was. He said no one should suffer like I had described and prepared me for the exam process I was about to endure. He left the room and I readied myself on the table. It was an interesting exam table made especially for examining rectums. I had never seen one of these before. He and his assistant came in to perform the exam. He was poking around in there and I almost came off the table. The pain was excruciating. I don't think either one of us expected it to hurt so badly. I was bleeding. I remember looking at his face and I immediately knew! It wasn't a hemorrhoid. It was something much worse.

I said to myself, "Oh my God. I have cancer and I'm going to die."

It was all I could do to breathe.

I asked, "What's wrong? What is it?"

He said calmly, "Please get dressed and I'll be back in a moment."

I wanted to scream, "Tell me now! Am I dying? What the hell is happening?"

I guess I was in shock. I did as I was told in a state of numbness and disbelief. Anal cancer? Rectal cancer? The only thing I knew at all about the subject was that Farrah Fawcett had had it and she'd died. Not very comforting thoughts.

When he came back in the room, his face told the story. He was quite somber. I tried to listen to what he was saying, but my mind was racing and I had so many questions. I remember he said, "It is *not* a hemorrhoid. We need to do a colonoscopy and biopsy to accurately determine what it is." My appointments were made on the way out the door at the receptionist desk and I stumbled out the door. I was attending the final class for my MBA. I made my appointment for a couple weeks out because I really needed to finish this class. It was the only thing standing between me and my master's degree that I had been working on for so many years. My first call was to my daughter and I honestly cannot even remember how it went. I tried to minimize the scare and protect her from what I was really thinking. The second call was to Andy, and I was standing in the hall at the hospital telling him about my doctor's visit. He was in Arkansas for work.

I told him, "I think I have cancer. I don't know what kind or how bad it is."

Obviously, there was nothing he could say or do. Nothing anyone could say or do. Andy and I had only been dating for a couple of years. I didn't really know what to expect, but I was positive supporting someone in a battle with cancer was not on his list of things he wanted to do. Early on, I told him he could leave. I knew this was not what he had signed up for when he started dating me and that he didn't owe me anything.

He just kept saying, "Whatever it is, we will get through it together." It was very comforting, even if I was not one hundred percent sure he meant it.

I got back to work and called my boss, Rick. I told him what had happened and that I would be needing a day off to do the colonoscopy in a few weeks. Rick had just survived his own battle with testicular cancer. He was a man of few words, but his actions were very powerful. He used his pull and scheduled me for a colonoscopy that Friday, then he came to my office to demand—well, convince me—that I should not wait. There would be another class and, yes, the degree might have to wait, but I needed to act immediately. I guess I knew he was right, but I didn't want to begin this journey.

Not even fifty years old yet, I had never had a colonoscopy. It wasn't due because I wasn't yet the recommended age to have one. I suffered through the miserable two-day prep and Andy took me early Friday morning for the procedure. Thanks to Versed and other medications, I had no recollection of the procedure and barely recall recovery. I vaguely remember my colorectal physician speaking to me and Andy. He handed us a picture and basically said, "I am sending the biopsy to pathology and will call you as soon as I get the results." The weekend felt like a month. It was a weekend I will never forget. Andy stayed with me, and we spent a lot of time looking at the picture and talking about the possibilities. You didn't have to be clinical to look at the photo and see the black cancerous tumor at the end of the rectum. I may not have known exactly what I was dealing with, but I had no doubt that it wasn't good.

At times I was inconsolable, crying and afraid. I kept saying, "I want to see my daughter grow up, get married, and have babies."

I thought about my own mother who had received a terminal cancer diagnosis at age fifty-eight. Her tears and sadness mainly surfaced when she thought about Jennifer and not seeing her grow up. Had I just been given a death sentence too? It was all so overwhelming. Not knowing my fate made it almost impossible to cope. What kind of cancer is it? Has it spread? Am I terminal? How long do I have? I also wondered if the chronic stress I had endured and my alcohol use were contributing factors.

Monday finally rolled around, and I went to work. Andy had to leave for a business meeting in Chicago. He didn't want to go, but life goes on and the surgeon had insisted the pathology could take a few days. I was struggling to stay focused on my job. One of my coworkers, Jamie, came into my office and her mere question, "How are you doing?" turned me into a blubbering mess. She decided then and there that I didn't need to be at work. She called Rick and told him we were taking a few days off. Next thing you know, Jennifer and her dog Freckman were on their way down for the road trip, along with my best friend Lexie. By the time the gang got loaded up in Jamie's van, it was close to 2 p.m. We had no plan or destination. We talked about going south, maybe to the beach, since it was my happy place. We had just started to head out of town when I received a call. It was the colorectal doctor's office. They had the results. Could I come in now? All heads were nodding yes. Jamie whipped the vehicle around and we headed back to the hospital. I was a nervous wreck. I was about to find out my fate. Thanks to Jamie and her spontaneous plan, I had my daughter by my side. If we hadn't decided to take this little excursion, I would have had to go it alone.

The visit was straightforward. The doctor said, "You have anal cancer."

I asked, "Is this the same cancer that killed Farrah Fawcett?

Jennifer wanted to get straight to the point and asked him directly, "Is my mom going to die?"

He said, "Yes, it is the same cancer that Farrah Fawcett had, but no, it doesn't mean you are going to die."

I heard everything he'd said but was unable to process much of it. There was still a lot we didn't know. Immediately, my life became a flurry of appointments. I needed an appointment to get a PET scan to see if it had spread. The tumor still needed to be staged. Another appointment was made with an oncologist and still another one with a radiation oncologist. It was overwhelming and surreal. There were more questions than there were answers at this point.

We joined Jamie and Lexie who were standing outside waiting for us with Freckman. I know Jennifer was trying to fill them in on what had just happened at the visit, but honestly, I just wanted a drink. We loaded back up in the minivan and headed down to Cocoa Beach. It was a time of discovery, drunkenness, and fear. I called Andy in Chicago and gave him the news. By the time we talked that evening, he, like every single one of us, had done some Google research on anal cancer. I was angry when I found that I had a stigma cancer. Are you kidding me? I had never even had anal sex and now I have anal cancer, which when googled pulls up things like it being associated with multiple partners, anal sex, and HPV. Andy was very upset when we spoke; he was convinced that he had given it to me, because of his "player" past. I was all too happy to blame him, someone, anyone. Was it my ex-husband? Was it Andy? Who had given it to me? I had only had sex with three men in the last thirty years. It had to be one of them. Or maybe my promiscuous past in my teens had caught up to me. Rick called me. He had done more than Google. He had spoken to some of the best oncologists on staff and he was excited to inform me that he thought my prognosis was good.

"You have a very curable type of cancer. You're one of the lucky ones," he said.

I didn't feel very lucky, but his words did give me hope. As I learned more about this rare cancer, STRESS is one of the major contributing factors. Living in fear and trepidation in an abusive marriage would certainly count as chronic stress. In typical Janet fashion, I pushed on without walking too far down the why me victim road.

The next day we floated around Discovery Cove. A mini vacation, fun time with Jennifer, Lexie, and Jamie before the onslaught of appointments and torturous treatment. I drank a lot and continued to cry, but the trip was an amazing gift to me. I will always be forever grateful for Jamie and Rick. They were both incredibly supportive and I don't know what I would have done without them.

Once we were back to Georgia and reality, I began learning exactly what was going to happen to me. Andy came with me to almost all of my appointments. In fact, he pretty much moved in and took care of me throughout the whole ordeal. My first physician appointment was with my radiation oncologist. He was very direct and spoke confidently. While he was examining me, he was asking me questions about my history and previous physician visits. I told him about the nurse practitioner examining me and saying I was full of stool. He actually cussed and said, "That is criminal." He was clearly angry that she had missed this tumor bulging into my vagina. I had a very pronounced rectocele. After the exam, he delivered the good news and the bad.

He said, "The good news is your PET scan was negative, meaning the cancer hasn't spread." He continued, boldly stating, "Your cancer is curable."

Well, that's good news—great news even. So what was the bad news?

He said, "The bad news is that the treatment for this cancer is brutal, but if you can make it through the treatment, you have a good prognosis."

If I make it through the treatment? What does that mean? Brutal? I needed thirty-three doses of radiation and two doses of chemotherapy. Radiation therapy was every day, Monday through Friday, until it was complete. I am really glad I didn't know how bad it would actually be.

I asked the usual questions about survival rate and long-term effects, then I asked a very important question: "Can I still drink alcohol?"

I was very relieved when he said, "Yes, you can still drink alcohol in moderation."

I chose not to think about the link between alcohol and cancer or the immune system. I was glad I didn't have to give up my wine. The physician likely already knew—what I would find out for myself soon enough—that I would have very little desire to drink once I was in the throes of this treatment.

The first few treatments were scary but non-eventful. I drove myself to the radiation center and then went to work. Jennifer had made arrangements to stay with me for the first week or so before she had to go off to grad school. Andy rearranged his work schedule as much as possible to be home and take me to treatment. We lined up people to come stay with me for the next few weeks. My ex-mother-in-law came for a week, Andy's mom came for a week, my Aunt J took a week, and my dad stayed a week. Jennifer came home when she could, but Andy was my primary caregiver. My sister wasn't really the caregiver type, although she did offer to come and stay. What she did was still very important: she sent me practical gifts like a blow-up donut to sit on, cool gel patches, and several other thoughtful items. She allowed me to call and cry and cuss. CC was the one person I could really open up and vent to. Everyone else was trying so hard to take care of me, I didn't want to seem disappointed or ungrateful, and I didn't want to let them down. When I talked with CC, I told her how miserable I was and shared my anger. She let me rant and rave but stayed calm and supportive. I had an excellent support system.

As the radiation began to take effect, it was unbearable. There was the relentless fatigue, but the worst part was the radiation burns. If you think about having radiation on a body part like your arm or breast, it would be bad and the burns would hurt, but imagine having to urinate and have bowel movements using the raw, radiated tissue every day. It was just about impossible. I remember at one point it felt like I was peeing razor blades it hurt so bad. My vaginal area looked like someone had filleted me with a knife. I tried all measures of comfort. Sitz baths, bathtub soaks, and a variety of creams. Sometimes the pain would be so bad I would just lie in the tub and cry. I even briefly thought about going underneath the water and ending the pain. Finally, my doctor prescribed me some Percocet. I took one and it was the first time since treatment that I didn't hurt. I am not one to take medicine and despise taking pills—rarely will I even take an Advil—but these pills were a life saver. Often Andy would have to beg me to take a pain pill. The flip side was you had to be careful not to take too much pain medicine for fear of constipation, which would be even more traumatic. Night after night I would be crying in pain, and he would get up in the middle of the night to run a bathtub for me. It was a horrible time. I couldn't go to work. I could barely walk. The chemotherapy was miserable. I had to have a port inserted and then the chemo bag was attached for several days. I developed mouth sores and didn't want to eat or even swallow.

Another thing that helped me through the experience was finding the website Blog for a Cure. It's a virtual support group where you can connect with people who have the same kind of cancer as you. I signed up and "met" a group of fellow anal cancer victims and survivors. I was able to post all of my questions, trials, and concerns. This wonderful group of men and women had such amazing advice and encouragement. Many of them had just finished their treatment or were going through it with me. What a blessing to be able to post a problem or symptom I was having and be bombarded with encouragement and advice. I learned about creams, medications, and survival tricks from the members of this site. I mourned when a fellow cancer victim was struggling with a relapse, pain, or lost their battle. It was an anonymous site, but I felt like I knew each one of these individuals.

Cancer changed me. I remember my first trip solo to the grocery store after months of being too weak to drive or carry groceries. It was a huge victory and helped me regain my sense of independence. I remember walking super slow and taking a long time to do even simple tasks. It was great to pick out what I wanted. My favorite brands and the bananas at the perfect ripeness for me. The little pleasures you take for granted, I was embracing and enjoying every single one. When I got up to the checkout, I was exhausted. My chemo brain and fatigue made it difficult for me to get my payment method together quickly. I noticed behind me a frustrated lady wondering why I was holding up the line and wishing I would get out of her way. At that moment, I realized how many times I had been that impatient lady, angry and frustrated at someone holding me up or wasting my time. Now it was me—struggling for strength both mentally and physically to make it through a basic task. To this day, I still try to remember that experience and when I am held up because someone is having a difficult time functioning, I remind myself that I don't know what they are going through. I need to give them grace. I have been there and don't know when I may be there again. When I got home with the groceries that day, I didn't have enough energy to put them away. I set them on the counter and headed for the couch to lay down, but I was delighted that I had successfully navigated a trip to and from the grocery store by myself. Remembering is good.

My cancer story has a very happy ending. I was able to dance with NED! Our lingo for the privilege of hearing the words, "no evidence of disease," aka NED. I have residual damage and will always have to deal with the side effects from radiation, but for the most part I live a normal, healthy life. I am truly one of the lucky ones. I am elated just to be cancer-free and grateful for my life. Another sobering reminder of the fragility of life.

ALL ABOUT THE BISCUITS

*A*ndy and I were now basically living together. He had really stepped up during my battle with cancer and was staying at my house most nights. He still had his own house, but he didn't spend much time there. We were really becoming a blended family. My only child enjoyed having the siblings she'd never had. She now claimed two brothers, Paul and Felix, even though she was off to graduate school and didn't get to see them all that much. Andy's oldest, Paul, was preparing to head off to college too. Felix was still around, so he spent a lot of time with us. We enjoyed boating on the lake, vacationing together, and spent all of our holidays together. It really is true that the hard times can bring people together.

I went back to work as soon as I was able. The folks at my job were truly wonderful and supportive during my treatment. Rick, having fought his own cancer battle, was especially empathetic. I really liked this position and the organization I was working for, but I was commuting almost an hour each way, into the city. Traffic was stressful and constant. Any accident or a rainy day could easily add an additional hour. Day by day it seemed to get worse. Once it took me three hours to get home. Honestly, I was struggling to justify wasting a minimum of two hours each day driving through frustrating traffic.

Cancer had changed my priorities and outlook on life. I was acutely aware of just how short and fragile life is. I'm not sure if my first taste of this fragility with my mother's death had lessened or been pushed aside, but here was another reminder of just how quickly your whole life can change. No one is promised tomorrow, so I really wanted to make the most of each day.

A few months later, as fate would have it, I got a call from someone I had worked with before. He had a VP position available with a large organization in Nashville. He described it as a great opportunity. The decision was a very hard one. I did love my job at the time and the supportive team I worked with. I told Rick about the opportunity, and he tried to get me to stay. I doubt I would have taken the new position if the commute had not been such a factor. My current organization even offered to move me to the city, but that was not for me. Andy and I discussed the position and what it would mean for us. Would he move with me, or would we try a long-distance relationship? What about Felix? Jennifer and Paul were off at college, but Felix was still at home, living nearby at his mom's. We decided I should go and at least interview for the position.

Long story short, I interviewed and was offered the job. The compensation package was lucrative and the growth potential unlimited. It was a whirlwind after that. Andy and I were committed to each other and basically made the decision together. I had decided to turn down the job if he didn't want to move. He had lived in his house with his kids near his ex-wife for many years. Andy decided to move with me, and I accepted the job offer. It was a stressful move. Neither of our houses sold due to the housing market at the time and we both ended up having to rent them out. We bought a big house in Nashville. The moving van literally went to my house and picked up all my stuff then went to his house and picked up all of his.

When all of our collective belongings were deposited into the house, it became real. We no longer had both my house and his—we had our house now. Luckily, the house was huge, and we found room enough for both sets of household goods. It was a challenging time for us, but we managed to adjust. My job was all-consuming, and I was working a lot of hours. I was learning the corporate environment and my new demanding role. It was all exciting, a new town with a ton of exquisite restaurants, live music everywhere, and so much to do. I was making the most money I had ever made and stepped right into that lifestyle. Andy, being an avid guitar player, loved Nashville. The kids visited us some and we made friends.

I'm not sure if it was all the first-rate restaurants, my stressful job, or our comfortable relationship, but I started gaining weight—we both did. It was all about the biscuits! I had already put on a little weight before we moved, but now it was getting out of control. Before I realized it, I was fat and miserable. I cried almost every morning when I was trying to find something to wear to work. I had dozens of beautiful, expensive suits that I had been wearing to work and now none of them fit. It was awful! I cannot even begin to tell you how much money I spent on clothes. I kept buying the next size up and the next size up. Most everything I wore was black to try and conceal my weight. I hated my body and my face so big and round with multiple chins. I constantly complained about how ugly and disgusting I was, yet I made no effort to change and, of course, I was drinking quite a bit.

We had a huge house party one night. Andy hired a musician friend of his to come and play. We had about thirty people there. It was so much fun. As always, I bought all the food and drinks—I loved playing hostess. I asked Jennifer to come help me with food as we teasingly call her Rachael Ray because of her wonderful culinary skills. She wrapped bacon around brussel sprouts, made macaroni-and-cheese balls, and prepared a gorgeous display of food. I very clearly remember the conversation we had that night in the kitchen. I was lamenting about my weight and bashing myself.

Jennifer looked at me and said, "Mom, I love you and I don't care how much you weigh, but I want you to be healthy and, honestly, if you're not happy with yourself, why don't you do something about it?" She continued, "You have the money. Hire a personal trainer."

What could I say? I don't think I even responded, but I thought about her statement. I had never been to a gym in my life—I didn't actually know what a personal trainer did. I was never athletic, had never played sports or lifted weights. I had done a few exercise classes and videos but never really worked out. There was no denying that I was miserable and something needed to change.

One morning, I was again trying to squeeze my now size fourteen body into one of my new size twelve suits and said enough is enough. My favorite stores like Ann Taylor and Banana Republic only carried clothes up to a size twelve. It was tough enough even finding that size. I knew the next step was going to a plus-size shop. My mom and sister had known and lived this struggle.

In desperation, I decided to see if I could find a personal trainer. In the next few days, I googled and called a few trainers nearby. The first guy I talked to told me I had to have a certain kind of heart monitor and that it was best to train in the morning. Ugh! I didn't want to get up at 5 a.m. and go train before going to work. That was discouraging. On my drive home one day, I noticed a Fitness Studio. I probably drove past it another week or two before I decided to drop in and see what they had to offer. I met the owner and told him I needed a personal trainer. I told him I had a demanding job and that after work would be the best time for me to come in. The owner introduced me to Darren, the afternoon and evening trainer. He was young and gorgeous. I found out later he was a former model. It absolutely didn't hurt that he was easy on the eyes. Maybe it even added a little extra motivation, I don't know. He told me it would just be me and him in the studio, which was a great comfort as the thought of going into one of those crowded gyms would have never worked for me. He also told me that if I did what he said, I could lose up to three pounds a week. Seriously? That sounded great! I had no idea what he was going to expect of me. I put off my start date until January. The day I was scheduled to start, I was sick as a dog and had to reschedule. Maybe the thought of this commitment was making me sick. The following week, I paid him a large sum of money and committed to six weeks. I decided I would try whatever he was advocating and see what happened. Paying the money had a way of keeping me committed.

My first session was rough. He measured me and weighed me, which was humiliating enough. He gave me two sheets of paper, one that listed foods to eat and the other foods to avoid. It was completely different from any other diet I had been on and, trust me, I have tried hundreds of diets over the years. Where were the rice cakes? Pretzels are good, right? No bread? No sweets? This guy must be nuts. Then he asked me to do these nearly impossible walking lunges across the length of the gym floor. The next day, I could barely get up or move. It seemed like the worst physical challenge I had ever done, and it was only day one. I whined and moaned, which didn't phase him. He told me in a few weeks I would be doing those lunges with weights. I seriously doubted that. But I had paid for six weeks. I was committed to this program and wanted to get my money's worth. This is one time in my life my "all or nothing" mentality worked to my advantage.

After each workout, I could hardly walk the next day. He had specific instructions on what I was to do when I was not working out with him two days a week. Walk, bike, take a class, or go to the gym on my "off days." I went home with my lists and cleaned out the refrigerator and the cabinets. Sorry Andy, no more Oreos or Pringles. I shopped and bought the items on the good list. I packed my lunch every day. I prepped food. I discovered healthier recipes and how to use herbs and spices. I didn't go out to eat. I even cut back on the alcohol. Yes, Darren said no alcohol, but I never completely quit.

Within two weeks, Andy had lost ten pounds. He just stopped eating the junk food I threw out and started eating my healthier dinners, and *he* loses ten pounds? How was that fair? I hadn't had a carb and had been working my ass off and managed to lose only six pounds. Seeing that I was beginning to lose weight was encouraging though. When I would come in, Darren would ask me about what I had been eating. Every session he would weigh me. He also shared cooking tips and ideas of healthy things to eat. This was his life—he knew all the tips and tricks. If I said I missed pizza, then he would tell me about cauliflower-crust pizza. Darren was committed to the lifestyle, and I was learning.

There were plenty of days I wanted to quit. I was sore and tired, but as the weight started dropping and the workouts progressed, I became more confident. Lucky for me, I fell in love with exercise and being active. I'm not sure how many months in it was, but I was feeling really good. I was back in my smaller sizes and feeling much more confident. I was probably back to my previous weight before the massive weight gain, maybe a hundred thirty pounds—back into a size eight and feeling good about myself. Darren weighed me and I was feeling so proud. He congratulated me on my progress and talked about pushing on.

Our next conversation has always stuck with me and quite frankly pissed me off. I said something about my weight being pretty good for someone my age and he said, "How much did you weigh in high school?" I told him about a hundred sixteen pounds.

He replied, "Well, you haven't gotten any taller."

I was so mad at him I wanted to quit, but I didn't, and I

continued to tone up and lose weight and feel fabulous. Within a few more months, I was wearing a size zero for the first time in my life. I couldn't believe it. The scale at one point hit almost one hundred fifteen pounds. I took a picture. I had lost over fifty pounds. People were complimenting and asking me what I had done. I constantly had people telling me I looked so much younger and healthier.

Finally, I was no longer fat! Surely that was the magic pill to make me happy, right? I had struggled with my weight and felt fat for so long. It is sad to admit, but one time when I was putting on a pair of size two jeans, I said to myself, "I feel fat." I had to remind myself that there is no possible way that someone fitting into a size two could be considered fat. My body image was so distorted.

You know how you never feel thin or pretty? You know how you always notice or see the things you hate about yourself? It is my chin for me. I hate my side profile. Plus, one of my eyes is bigger than the other. Why is it so easy to focus on our flaws? Worse yet, you look back at pictures when you were younger or thinner and say, I guess I didn't look that bad back then, but look at me now. Never satisfied with ourselves, never good enough. It must stop!

I was jazzed about my weight loss. Buying size two and zero clothes was so much fun. People started saying things like, "You don't need to lose any more weight," and, "You are going to blow away." I even had someone refer to me as the skinny girl—now that was a first! It was rewarding, but it was a full-time job and obsession. I went to the gym seven days a week. I didn't eat out. Period. I would not touch a bite of cake or a cookie, not even at birthdays, holidays, or parties. Controlling my diet and exercise was a priority in my life. Andy lost weight too. He was not nearly as obsessed as me, but he lost over fifty pounds. He had played ball in school and had a fitness history. It was easy for him to jump back into an active lifestyle. We went to the gym together, hiked, biked, and swam.

I made a photo album of our weight gain and weight-loss journey. On the back there is a picture of me in a bikini jumping into the air. The caption says, "Nothing tastes as good as fit feels." If only it was all so easy as a slogan. If only we were perfect and consistent. One thing I know is that happiness is not based on a number on the scale. Finding balance and moderation has always been difficult for me. I will likely always be tempted by a biscuit or a vanilla angel donut (the powdered sugar donut with white cream filling), but I will keep pushing toward my goal of health and fitness.

CUMULATIVE GRIEF

My sister CC and I were always very different. She and I fought like cats and dogs when we were younger. Although I was the older sister, in many ways it was my sister who was protective of me. I don't know if I was just self-absorbed or if all kids are like this, but when she copied my every move, I hated it. My little sister always wanted to tag along, and I wanted my independence. When my dad left, my sister was somewhat of a lost child: nine years old and somehow fending for herself.

As we got older our differences got bigger. I married young and moved away. She lived with Mom, and when she did move out, it was only a few miles down the road. I think she may have been jealous of me—maybe because I was thinner or older or maybe because of her own issues. I always loved my sister and there was never a time in my life that we were not connected. I knew I could call her at any time and she would drop whatever she was doing to be there for me. I'm ashamed to say that I was not always the same for her. My life was consumed with Fred, Jennifer, religion, and career. I was always busy or preoccupied with something. We still made time to see each and got together often. We rarely went more than a few days without at least talking on the phone, and boy could my sister talk! I remember one time after I'd left Fred, I was driving home from a weekend trip at my dad's house. It was a six-hour drive. I called CC once I got on the road and we literally talked until I turned into my driveway. I laughed and said, "Well, thanks for making the trip home with me."

I have no idea what we talked about for six solid hours, but my sissy was rarely at a loss for words. We were much closer after I got away from Fred. I was free to visit and develop our relationship more. I was drinking more and that also seemed to unite us. CC drank a lot.

My sister had a heart of gold and was generous to a fault. She was also outspoken and full of life. She had so many friends. CC bought her house when she was twenty-three years old and was very proud of that accomplishment. She never lived anywhere else. She always struggled to make ends meet, but she never asked for a handout or expected anyone to help. She was super smart and incredibly talented. We all wanted her to go to college, but she never did. Once she took a massage therapist course, and I swear she learned more about anatomy than I did in nursing school. Her memory was sharp, a gift I never had. Before she was able to graduate, she hurt her back and had to drop out. It was such a shame. CC gave the most wonderful massages. I am positive she would have been an excellent therapist. I can feel her hands on my neck now, as I think back to her impromptu massages. She would make such a fuss about how tense, knotted, and tight I was. She would say, "Janet, I don't know how you can walk around like this, with all this stress."

I guess I was just used to it. One of her greatest assets was her creativity. She came up with all sorts of business ideas, wrote jingles and slogans, and made cards. She helped me (the college graduate) set up my rental condo website and came up with the catchy name Bucket List Beach Condo.

My sister struggled with her weight her entire life, like my mom. I suppose it's a family thing. We all struggled with weight, but CC had confidence. I remember telling her one time how I wished I could have just a little of that self-confidence she so effortlessly displayed. She was a beautiful lady and carried herself well. She had big striking brown eyes and a seductive smile. CC wore her hair in an eighties style with long straight brown hair down her back and blown back bangs. Her peace sign earrings and natural beauty came and went in and out of style, but she never wavered. My sister never lacked for male attention either. She had plenty of men friends and even some marriage proposals, but she never let herself fall that hard. She often said that she would never love someone as much as my mom loved my dad, and she didn't. When someone would get too close, she would push them away.

Going to my sister's house was like stepping back into the eighties. In addition to her hairstyle and fashion, she was a collector of things. Her house was filled with the things she loved. Collectible telephones, signs, candles, masks, and some really cool eighties memorabilia. After mom's death, CC took a lot of my mom's belongings and displayed them as well. Pot smoke, records, and collectibles were everywhere. CC was not the best house-keeper, but when she knew I was coming for a visit, she would do what she called "the flight of the bumblebee" and buzz around frantically cleaning up. CC always had a difficult time making herself do things she didn't want to do, so oftentimes she just didn't.

It was a running joke in our family about how many W-2s she would have in a year. She never seemed to have any trouble getting a job, but somehow within a few months (or even sooner) something would always go wrong at the organization. Personality conflicts, financial issues, and all kinds of intriguing stories about why she hated the job and needed to quit. In fact, almost every single company she worked for ended up closing. It was probably because of her field, being a bookkeeper and gal Friday, she was attractive to the smaller business-like mom-and-pop shops, but we joked that if you hired CC, you may not stay in business long. We had a lot of laughs about her job antics. There were a couple jobs she really liked though. She managed and basically ran those offices for several years, but the other short-term jobs in between were more than interesting. One year, I think she had twelve jobs.

One of my favorite stories was from a company she'd been working at for about three months—she hated that job. I got the all-too-familiar call, "Janet, I hate this job. I feel sick in the morning thinking about having to go. I'm miserable. Do you think I should quit?"

Of course, she just wanted me to say yes and after the first few attempts at reasoning or trying to help her work out the actual issues, I decided my approval was all she really wanted. I would say, life is too short, just quit, you'll get another job. Well, this particular company apparently loved her and, as she told it, wouldn't let her quit.

I said, "They can't make you stay, CC."

She said, "You call them, Janet, and tell them I quit."

I agreed to the strange request. I called the company and told them who I was. I made up some story about CC coming to live with me or something. The lady said, "No, she needs to come to work. We need her."

I said, "Well, I'm sorry, but she's not coming back."

I swear, the lady argued with me for twenty minutes. She didn't want to let her quit. CC and I laughed about that encounter forever.

I loved going to my sister's house, especially after my mom died. It was like the one place that was stable, consistent, always there. Despite our differences, we were very close. I loved my sissy (as I called her) with all my heart. Looking back, I wish I would have spent more time with her and been a better sister, but those are just more worthless regrets.

One day, I felt a strange knot in my neck. I was worried. I saw a doctor, had imaging done, and was waiting for the results. It turned out to be nothing. A few days later, CC called me and said, "Sis, I think I am having sympathy pains. My lymph nodes in my neck are swollen this morning."

She asked if I thought she should go to the doctor. I said, "Yes, something is going on, probably best to get it checked out."

She went to a walk-in clinic and they told her to go to the emergency room because she needed to get imaging done. The ER doctor did a chest CT and then told her to follow up as soon as possible with her primary care doctor.

He handed her the CT results and said, "Make an appointment right away, and take this to your doctor."

I will never forget, I was driving home from work when she called to tell me what was happening. I was surprised they had given her the report. I asked her to read it. She started reading: "Suspect metastatic disease, further imaging is required."

I almost ran off the road.

She said innocently, "What does that mean, Sissy?"

I could barely speak. I just said, "Send me a picture of the report. I need to look at it. I'm almost home."

What the fuck? You give someone a paper that tells them they likely have cancer that has spread? I got the report and I couldn't believe it. It had to be wrong! And just like that, I was in the middle of a terrible déjà vu. We talked a little that night about what it could be, and she promised to call her primary care doctor in the morning. Luckily, at that time, I was only living about two hours from her house. I was able to make it to many of her appointments. Thankfully, she also had a great support system of close friends.

The day of her first appointment with the oncologist, I drove over and took her to the appointment. They had assigned her to a doctor halfway across town. He was supposed to have the biopsy results. We went in and he was very casual.

He said, "You have cancer, and we need to start chemotherapy on Monday."

I said, "Where are the pathology reports? What kind of cancer is it? Where has it spread?"

He said he didn't have the results back and I nearly lost it. He said, "It's probably lymphoma, since so many of your lymph nodes are involved."

"Probably?" I asked. "I drove all the way over to get these results. You think you're going to start my sister on a chemotherapy regimen, and you don't even know what kind of cancer she has?" My voice was raised, and he knew I wouldn't be leaving there without the results. I continued, "The biopsy was done a week ago. Where are the results?"

He left the room. My sister looked at me and said, "I'm so glad you are here."

He came back in and was much more somber. "It's lung cancer," he said. "It has spread to multiple sites."

CC was sitting in the chair, and I was standing beside her holding her hand. She looked up at me with her big brown eyes. She looked like a twelve-year-old girl looking up at her mommy for comfort and assurance. I will never forget that look. Her eyes said, "What does he mean?" They pleaded to know, "Am I going to die?" Her bewildered look, searching for answers to the question.

"What are we going to do?" she asked.

I simply held her and said, "We're going to walk through this together."

I moved her care to another physician, one we both liked much better. The new office was closer to her house, so getting to therapy was more convenient. Coincidentally, it was the same place my mom received cancer treatment. I was watching a rerun of the most horrific story I'd ever seen and hoping—praying—for a different outcome, though I knew it was unlikely.

The next ten months were a blur. I had just accepted a job. The position was a little farther from my sister's house but also offered me more flexibility. I drove to CC's almost every weekend and attended as many appointments as I could. We talked every day, sometimes two or three times a day. We spent quality time together, just me and my sissy. One day we were talking about things she wanted to do, things on her bucket list. She said, "I've always wanted to go to New York." Two weeks later, we were at the Crowne Plaza in the middle of Times Square with Aunt J and Lexie. Anything she asked for, I tried to get her. One day she laughingly said, "You're better than the Make-A-Wish Foundation." Unfortunately, there were only a handful of trips or requests. She had always been a homebody and, as her health declined, all she wanted to do was stay home with her doggie. Faithful friends stopped by morning, noon, and night. Her home became my home away from home. I cherished every visit but couldn't stand the pain of what was happening. I was drinking a lot to help me cope.

After our mom died, we'd started an annual tradition called Dee Day. There were eight of us: my Aunt J, Aunt Mimi, Annie (my mom's best friend), Bon, (Annie's sister), CC, Raeray, (CC's best friend), Jennifer, and me. Every year we would get together, rent a house, and celebrate my mom's life. For sixteen years, we never missed a year. It was a time of reminiscing. We told stories, shared pictures, and kept her memory alive. Our annual Dee Day celebration was looming and we all knew it would be my sister's last. We invited my cousin Jane. She was not an original member of the group, but she and CC were very close. Jane said she couldn't come because she couldn't get off work. Then out of the blue, after working with her current organization for over twelve years, they suddenly decided to let her go. It was a sign—Jane was meant to come to Dee Day. We had no idea what an important role she would play in this whole situation. It was a different Dee Day, but it was special. CC was extremely sick and didn't get out to the beach much. On the day we were leaving, she wanted to see the ocean one last time. We walked hand and hand out on the boardwalk to see the ocean. How thankful I am Jane captured the moment in a photo. I will forever cherish that picture and the time we spent there.

When Jane drove CC back to her house, she knew she needed to stay. Losing her job was the biggest blessing any of us could have asked for. Jane decided she would stay in Florida and be with CC until the end, and she lived there with CC for the next two and a half months until she died. I sometimes wonder if I should have quit my job and stayed with my sister, but I think I was too close. I don't know if it would have been for the best. When I was around my sister, she put on a brave front and focused on me—she always had. Jane and CC managed the day-to-day care, and I visited almost every weekend. I stayed for as many appointments as I could.

There was nothing left unsaid between me and my sissy. We talked, laughed, and cried for many hours. I must have apologized a dozen times for not being a good big sister, but she would always say the same thing: "Janet, you made me stronger. You made me who I am today."

She didn't have any anger, and she loved me unconditionally. I never felt closer to my sister in my life. She was genuinely worried about leaving me, and she would often say, "I'm sorry I'm going to leave you alone in this world."

Our dad was still alive, but the truth is he had very little recollection of our childhood or past. He remarried and built his new life with Bertha. Although we both love our daddy very much, it felt like just me and my sissy most of the time. He never spent holidays or events with us. It was always his new family, a fact that didn't really bother me, but which CC strongly resented. I guess she knew what I was about to find out about cumulative grief. Every loss adds to the previous one and can overwhelm you. It was also awful to watch my dad experience every parent's worst nightmare. I can think of nothing worse than losing a child. I was losing my sister, but my dad was watching his youngest daughter die.

Even with death looming, we managed to laugh a lot. I remember going through some of her stuff—man, did she have a lot of stuff—and finding a pile of wigs. We tried each one on and took pictures. CC upstaged me as usual. She rocked the wig in the photo, but I looked like a big goof. We laughed hysterically. I kept trying to throw things away, knowing soon I would be left with all of it, but she couldn't part with any of it. When we were sorting through her ornaments after Christmas, I knew it was hopeless. We had three piles: one for trash pile, one to donate, and another to keep. The keep pile was huge, and the trash had almost nothing in it. I picked up an old Santa Claus with a broken arm and said, "Now surely this can go in the trash pile," but she tried to convince me that someone may want it and to just put it in the give-away pile.

That was it! We didn't bother sorting anything else. She went through the things she wanted me, her friends, or other family members to have, but there weren't enough hours left to deal with all of her possessions. None of it really mattered anymore anyway.

Jane called me about five days before my sister died. I had just been there two days prior and was planning to return that weekend, but she told me things had gotten worse and I needed to come that day. I was preparing for an important board meeting that night at my new job. I had only been working there for less than six months, but I said, "I have to go." I think the five-hour drive took me about four. I didn't know what to expect.

When I got there, to Jane's amazement, my sister popped up and said, "What are you doing here today?"

She seemed about the same to me. Jane told me it was the first time in days she had shown any spunk and assured me this was not at all the way she'd been behaving. We all knew the end was near, but no one knew exactly when that would be. By the next day, it was easy to see what Jane was saying. CC was barely eating, and it was becoming much more painful and challenging for her to get up and down. When the hospice nurse visited that day, we had a candid conversation, and she was certain death was only a few days away.

The vigil began. I knew she needed to get a hospital bed because it was becoming impossible for her to get in and out of her own bed. I also knew that trying to get her to the bathroom was becoming more and more dangerous. Her femur was riddled with cancer—it was miraculous she was still walking at all. We could not risk a fall. I ordered a hospital bed, and she was not the least bit happy about it. I remember pushing her wheelchair from the bathroom to the living room where the hospital bed sat. She was exhausted. It was a workout for Jane, CC, and I just to transfer her from the commode to the wheelchair. I explained to Sissy that this was going to keep her more comfortable and make it easier for her to get up and down. I knew I was lying, and she knew it too. We all knew she was getting into her deathbed.

Jane and I tried to lift her from the chair to the bed, but it was not happening. I asked Jane to hold the chair and I bent down to lift CC up. She said, "No, Janet," and with whatever ounce of energy she had left, she pushed herself up out of the chair.

We quickly moved her to the bed and then got her situated. Seeing her lying in that hospital bed was so excruciating. I had to convince her to get a catheter. She simply wasn't strong enough to get in and out of bed on her own. I sat by her bed. We all did. She was alert, but her breathing was becoming somewhat labored, and it took almost too much effort for her to talk. She did tell me she loved me. I'm not sure if those were her last words to me, but I like to think they were.

Dad and Bertha were there. Jane was there. Aunt J, Lexie, and Jennifer came. CC's friends cycled through day and night. Her neighbors visited with food for us. Jane and I slept on the loveseat and sofa in the living room next to her hospital bed. We set the alarms to give her morphine around the clock to keep her pain-free. After three days, we were emotionally and physically exhausted. I started to wonder how much longer she could live like this. Could it be weeks? I also started wondering how long Jane and I could keep going.

CC's dog Shadow, her faithful companion, never left the bedside. We sang, prayed, talked to CC. We hugged her, rubbed her, played her favorite music. Another day passed. Was it night or day? Had any of us eaten or showered? We were absorbed with her care. She was restless and began thrashing around. She moaned and I found it unbearable. I called the hospice nurse and demanded they do something. How can we be more humane to animals than we are to our loved ones? Why do we let them suffer? Jane and I upped the morphine. We added some Valium, whatever the hospice nurse had given us. I stayed a moderate level of drunk most of the day. Jane smoked her weed. We teased CC, saying she had the best care on the planet. A drunk nurse and a stoned caregiver. She laughed at us and said she loved it. Now she was just there existing. She was only fifty years old, her heart and other organs still strong and fighting for survival, the cancer slowly eating away at her lungs, bones, and lymphatic system.

My sissy died five days after she was moved to the hospital bed. She was pronounced dead at 4:20 p.m. I wonder if that was fate. It made us all smile. The overwhelming grief and sadness set in. Plans were in place, with cremation and an estate company to help with the items in the house. As soon as she died, the house felt cold and empty. Her poor doggie was in mourning. He wouldn't even move. I thought he had died right along with her. It was another very dark day in my life.

Jane took Shadow and, somehow, we all went back to our own lives. The hole in my heart from losing my mom was even bigger now with my sister gone. And she was right—it felt worse, more unfair. I felt even more alone. I wasn't sure I would ever be happy again, but life doesn't stop after death. Alcohol was there to numb and console me. CC gave me Jane, and what we went through together bonded us like sisters. She moved into my inner circle and became such an important part of my life. Jennifer found out she was pregnant during CC's illness, and the circle of life continued.

ENDING ANOTHER ABUSIVE RELATIONSHIP

*A*s I hit my fifties, I had to look around and admit what a wonderful life I had. A close relationship with my beautiful daughter and her family, and a wonderful husband that loves me just the way I am. Yes, I married Andy.

I'm educated and I have a successful career, a beautiful place to live, and lots of wonderful friends. I get to be my social self, host parties, and surround myself with family and friends, yet something still seemed to be missing.

Throughout my sister's battle with cancer and after she died, I found solace in alcohol. The cumulative grief I was feeling was indeed overwhelming. I was eating bad, gaining weight, and did not care. My nightly glass of wine had gradually become two or three. It wasn't particularly alarming and didn't seem excessive. Everyone around me was drinking too, right? After all, I had a stressful high-level job, worked every day, no DUI, no financial issues, and I had recently suffered the loss of my sister. My family and friends thought I was fine. I was a happy drunk for the most part and seemed to be enjoying myself. Still, a small voice inside said, "This can't be healthy." Despite researching articles about the benefits of alcohol and trying to convince myself my alcohol intake was normal, I knew it wasn't.

I honestly never even considered attending an event, activity, or establishment that didn't allow alcohol and barely ever had to. I drove home after a couple glasses of wine way more times than I care to remember. In fact, it was becoming clearer that there was a lot I couldn't remember. I would look at my phone to see who I had texted or called the night before. I would have a conversation with my hubby, and he would say we'd talked about it the night before.

One weekend we were visiting friends and my husband videotaped me and my girlfriend having a hilarious conversation after who knows how many bottles of wine. There I was, slurring my words, talking, and laughing, but the next day when I saw the video, I couldn't believe it. I had no recollection of that conversation. Those incidences happened too often. I began to realize just how integrated alcohol was in my life. I owned all the alcohol paraphernalia, the "you had me at merlot" shirts, personalized wine glasses, wine cooler, "bring me wine" socks and flip flops, an extensive cork collection, plaques, and signs about it being wine time or five o'clock somewhere—I even had a huge liquor cart. I was happy to be surrounded by alcohol. It comforted me when I was grieving, helped me cope with my stressful life, and was there for all my celebrations. Why would I quit?

I woke up around 3 a.m. almost every night, dehydrated and regretful. I made empty promises of not drinking anymore, cutting back, and changing my relationship with alcohol. I bought a heart monitor to be sure my heart rate of 144 in the middle of the night was not a fatal rhythm. My weight was up, my eyes and face were puffy, and most days I felt a moderate level of fatigue. I began googling, "how do you know if you're an alcoholic?" and even mentioned to my therapist that I might be drinking too much. Our society is very generous about drinking habits and you can easily find articles, friends, and proof to convince yourself that you're fine. Most mornings I would wake up and swear I wasn't going to drink that night. I even wrote myself notes before I went to bed that read "no ETOH," a medical term and the abbreviation for the chemical compound ethanol, or ethyl alcohol. But, of course, I'd end up stopping by the liquor store on my way home.

If I knew there was only one bottle of wine at the house, sometimes I would drink a beer or vodka first to be sure one bottle would be enough. To get off the wine, I tried switching to vodka and cranberry juice, but after a couple of drinks I just craved wine and ended up opening a bottle anyway. Many mornings, I would get up and go to the fridge to see if I left any wine in the bottle. A good day was when there was a little left in the bottom of the bottle. I have a lot of frightening stories I don't really want to remember, and a ton of regrets. I said and did things under the influence I would never have said or done sober. I ate badly, didn't sleep well, snored, gained weight, and spent a lot of money on booze. Most days, I felt a general sense of malaise that I thought was normal. I knew I was drinking a lot more since my sister's death. I guess I thought it was helping me cope.

The year after my sister's death, Jennifer had my first grand-baby. She was the light of my life. I never thought I would be one of those "let me tell you about my grand-kids" grandmas, but I am the worst. When Olivia was only eight months old, Houston, my son-in-law, got a job offer in my town. He took the position and moved the family here. I couldn't have been happier. I knew I wanted to spend as much time as I could with this sweet baby. The timing was perfect, as I was completely burnt out with my healthcare leadership role and ready for a break.

I quit my six-figure job with no plan other than to decompress and spend more time with my family. This afforded me the opportunity to watch my sweet grand-daughter a couple days a week. The more time I spent with her, the more I began to think of my energy level and longevity. Sometimes she would spend the night with me and Andy. After she was in bed, I would pour a glass of wine and then another. I began to worry that, if something happened in the middle of the night, would I be able to drive? Would I be capable of making a good decision? Could I take care of this precious baby? I decided I needed to cut back, but making the decision to reduce my alcohol intake was what really shocked me. The more I told myself I wouldn't drink, the more I drank. Moderation was painful. You can have one glass tonight; don't drink today; maybe a beer and one glass of wine later tonight— always bargaining with myself and negotiating. I was never satisfied with just one drink though.

I had seen the Facebook advertisement for One Year No Beer many times. It kept popping up with pictures and posts of people saying how much better their life was without alcohol. One day, I decided to give the OYNB twenty-eight-day challenge a try and see what happened. I bought the book and signed up. I basically white knuckled through twenty-eight days of sobriety.

"Yay," I told myself, "I'm not an alcoholic. Now I can go back to drinking."

And boy did I—more than ever. The twenty-eight-day challenge ended two days before my annual Girls' Weekend with Lexie, Sophie, and ToriJill. I drank so much the first night of our weekend that I threw up. We had to cancel plans the next day so they could nurse me back to life. The girls were sweet and understanding, and we all made excuses about how my tolerance level was down from not drinking. I had been drinking a Hippie Punch with mixed liquors, so I was quick to blame that. Even as much as I tried to convince myself, I couldn't stop thinking that it was not okay. The more I tried to cut back or moderate, the more I drank. I would drink a shot of tequila before going out to eat so I wouldn't have to wait for a drink. Was I an alcoholic? I couldn't be. I never drank in the morning or even during the day, unless it was vacation or the weekend, so I certainly didn't have a drinking problem.

Vacations were meant for drinking. The days started with mimosa mornings, followed by beer afternoons that ended with wine nights. Lots of stories, lots of red flags, but I enjoyed drinking—I deserved it. The thought of quitting was not an option. I just needed to get it under control. Honestly, I didn't drink any more than any of my friends. Everywhere I looked, alcohol consumption was deemed normal and, besides, who doesn't drink?

But since I had joined OYNB, I knew that there was a group of people who didn't drink. They posted pictures of their transformations and talked about being on the "fun side of the island." These people seemed happy and relieved they were no longer drinking. I rocked on, denying that I was struggling internally with my desire to cut back or quit drinking. I frequently asked my friends and family if they thought I drank too much, but they couldn't decide for me. How could they possibly know how I felt inside? On the outside I was so put together. Plus, I was fun, right? The life of the party. There had to be at least a little fear that if I quit, all the parties and good times would end.

I continued drinking, eating badly, and feeling tormented. My struggle with moderating alcohol made me feel powerless and weak. It became clearer and clearer that I had to do something. I decided to try the OYNB ninety-day challenge starting January 1, 2019. It was different this time. I signed up for the private Facebook group and read everything I could get my hands on about quitting alcohol. They call it "quit lit"—Annie Grace's *The Naked Mind*, *Alcohol Explained* by William Porter, and many others. As I read these books, I felt relief. Turns out I'm not a weak-willed individual who just can't moderate; rather, alcohol is a highly addictive poison that we are being seductively marketed into believing makes us feel good and relieves stress.

The truth about what alcohol does to your brain and body is not commonly discussed, but the facts are shocking. Alcohol dehydrates you, increases your chance of several types of cancers, causes liver disease, reduces concentration, escalates anxiety, and decreases metabolism, just to name a few. How could something legal, mainstream, and so highly promoted by our culture be that bad? Oh wait—flashback to the days when cigarettes where mainstream and promoted by our culture. People smoked everywhere. They smoked cigarettes on television, in restaurants, and even in hospitals. The tobacco company advertised everywhere and hired macho men and sexy women to promote the product. It wasn't until society put pressure on the tobacco industry to make public what they already knew—that their product was killing people. It took many years and a lot of grassroots advocates to break through and change the status of smoking.

Drinking is now where smoking was then. The social pressure of drinking is real. It is the only addiction I know of that, when you try to quit, people want to know why. They act like something is wrong with you and either try to convince you to at least have just one or feel sorry for you because you must be a bad alcoholic. Can you imagine announcing to your family you're going to give up an addiction like cocaine and having them try to convince you to just cut back? Maybe just do a line now and then? Ridiculous! Not with alcohol though. People think you're extreme if you want to completely quit drinking. What a pity to be a problem drinker—an alcoholic.

"Alcoholic" is such a negative label. The mental image of the unshaven, disheveled guy on the park bench holding his brown bagged bottle in his hand immediately pops into my mind. What is an alcoholic? Who is an alcoholic? Not me. The term alcoholic is no longer used. It is now alcohol use disorder. You can find different ranges of acceptable use, but it varies: anywhere from five to seven drinks a week for women and up to fourteen for men.

Regardless of how much you drink, everyone agrees giving your brain and body a break from alcohol is worthwhile. When you choose to quit drinking you have to be prepared for the onslaught of well-meaning people asking why in the world you would give it up. Others will try desperately to convince you that just one won't hurt you. I understand. I get it. I was a drink pusher myself. I felt better when everyone around me was drinking. Even my family and friends questioned why I needed to completely stop drinking.

Socializing stopped for a while. Most of my friends were drinkers and I was not ready to be around them. I turned down several invites but tried to stay in touch in other ways. I honestly didn't know what kind of activity I could do that didn't involve drinking alcohol. The thought of going to a bar was out of the question. I had to attend a few work dinners with wine flowing and it was too painful. The first few weeks without alcohol were brutal. I'm not kidding. I went to bed at 8:30 several nights. I moped around feeling deprived of my faithful companion, my best friend. Other times I became down-right angry. My moods and emotions were all over the place. I cried a lot. The grief I had suppressed or numbed with alcohol was now engulfing me. It was a tough thirty days, then sixty days. It is a wonder I didn't get fired or divorced.

I posted on the OYNB private Facebook page and received a ton of support. It was like I was being submerged in a secret anti-drinking culture and I longed to be surrounded by these like believers. I needed to read the encouraging posts of how it would get better. I needed to be reassured that the cravings would not last forever. It helped to hear that I was not weak—alcohol is just extremely addictive and powerful. While the physical cravings were tough, the bigger struggle for me was dealing with the raw emotions buzz-free. Grief, anxiety, regret, frustration, and even happy feelings were all previously handled with a drink. Now when these emotions and situations arose, it was just me totally sober, trying to cope. I felt every tinge of anger and every hint of fear. My grief, disappointment, and worry were at times unbearable. The quit lit and my new sober friends promised me that this was all normal. I had to trust the others who had traveled down this road and believe it would eventually pass, but I felt like a crazy woman, out of control.

As the days, weeks, and months went by, my body began to feel healthier. My chronic low-level fatigue lifted. My eyes brightened and the puffiness went away. Even though I was eating poorly, I lost some weight. Turning to sugar was a short-term fix I would have to address later on. I found more time to exercise. In fact, I had a lot more time. Previously, my typical evening had me pouring my first glass of wine no later than seven in the evening, sometimes earlier. By eight o'clock, there was no way I was able to drive anywhere. Now, without booze, I can go somewhere and actually drive myself home. What a revelation. My resting heart rate went from the eighties to the fifties. I slept through the night. I woke up without regrets or fear of what had happened the night before. I stopped having diarrhea. Ha! I thought it was a chronic condition leftover from my cancer treatment. Turns out it was just the booze. My hair got shinier. People started commenting that I looked younger and that something about me was different. The physical changes were a bonus.

I will have to say that not drinking got a little easier with time. I stayed close to the tribe and kept up my reading. There were days when something would happen or I would get triggered, and it took real willpower or support from sober peers to keep me from drinking. I came pretty close a couple of times and I can't count how many cravings I fought off. Then around day seventy-two when I was pretty much out of the habit of drinking every night, a strong craving hit me like a wave. I wanted to drink so bad that day—the whole day. I even thought about stopping at a bar at lunch, which I never did on a weekday. I didn't cave, but it shook me up. I realized alcohol still had a strong pull for me.

The ninety-day challenge would be ending soon, and I struggled with what to do next. I knew I wasn't ready to be on my own. I still needed support or I would go right back to drinking because moderation alludes me. The truth is, if I could have cut back on my drinking, I would never have joined this group. I didn't want to sign up for three hundred sixty-five days—that seemed like too much of a commitment—but as the ninety days grew closer, I knew I needed to go forward with OYNB for the year. With some encouragement from my fellow OYNB members, I upgraded my goal to three hundred sixty-five days.

On day one-fifty or maybe one-seventy, something magical happened. I was in the hot tub with my hubby—he had a mixed drink and I had my water. I realized for the first time ever I was not envious of his drink. I wasn't sitting there wishing I could have a drink too. I didn't want to drink! I was so excited. It felt like a major victory and freedom. Don't get me wrong, I have had other cravings and temptations to drink, but something changed for me that day. My original goal was to do as much time sober as I needed to break the tolerance cycle, then get back to drinking socially and moderating my intake. But why? Why should I bring alcohol back into my life?

Flash forward now to over three years alcohol-free. Not one sip or blip. At the one-year anniversary of no alcohol, I asked myself the question: Are you going to go back to drinking? I still have not said never, but what I have said is why would I? What would be the benefit to adding poison back to my life? Occasionally I will think about having a drink, but it's never because I love the taste or miss drinking. It's because I have had a shit day or something is stressing me out and I want to call up my old reliable friend to numb the feeling. Of course, I know that is the moment I least need to drink. I usually play it forward and think about how I will feel if I give in, and the thought is fleeting.

Today my granddaughters get a fully present, completely sober grandma. My friends and family are spending time with the real Janet—sober Janet—the way God made me. Imperfect and with all my flaws but completely unindulgent. I have learned to laugh and enjoy social settings without booze. I am often the odd woman out, refusing to imbibe, but that's okay. Quitting alcohol is the best gift I have ever given myself and those that love me. Giving it up was only the beginning. I asked myself, "If I can do hard things like this, what else can I do?" And the plunge into my personal development continued.

PART II

SECOND HALF OF LIFE

*a*s I roll into the second half of life, I keep asking myself the burning question, "What do I want to do when I grow up?" With the years flying by, I feel a strong urge to find the answer fast. After putting down the alcohol and sorting through the raw emotions, I began an intense journey of self-development. I struggled my entire life with self-esteem issues and, despite the accomplishments, therapy, and my belief that God loves me, I continue to torment myself with "Janet hating" and negative self-talk. I have gotten better at recognizing the futility of this action, but controlling my thought pattern is difficult.

* * *

"Comparison is the thief of joy."

— - C. S. LEWIS

I WOULD THINK of what I really wanted to do in life, but my limiting beliefs kept holding me back. I wanted to write a book, to share my passion of healthy living and freedom from alcohol, but the nagging doubt that I was not good enough or smart enough kept plaguing me. What could I possibly share with a world full of people smarter, funnier, more interesting than me? If you are anything like me, it's easy to compare yourself to others. It often appears that everyone else is perfectly happy and doing better than you. I remember when I first started going to church, I looked at the other families there and thought how lucky they all were. There I was living in my messed up, toxic marriage barely coping, and everyone else seemed to have such happy, put-together families. It wasn't until I got to know some of the families more intimately that I realized they were all struggling, and not one of them was as perfect as they appeared.

Just look at any social media page. People post all smiles, travel, and bliss. I'm guilty of this myself. I wish my real life looked more like my Facebook page. Every post is filled with pictures of great vacations, time with friends, family, and accomplishments. Almost every single picture I've ever posted shows me wearing a smile. Do I really smile that much? Am I always happy? Is my life complete bliss? Well, I do tend to be a mostly positive person but, let's face it, my Facebook page is nowhere near reality. Yes, they are all real pictures of me doing fun stuff and having a great time, but they only represent a small portion of my real life. Most days are not documented for all to see. I look back at the year I had cancer and see very few picture posts. I did reach out and ask for prayers, but there were not many happy smiling pictures or exciting events to share. I was basically trying to get through the brutal treatment and praying that I wouldn't die.

No, things are not always as they appear. If only our minds gave us reality instead of our own filtered messages. I cannot tell you how many times I was absolutely convinced that someone didn't like me because they didn't respond in the way I expected. Social media has made it worse. It's easy to get sucked into the never-ending questions. How many likes did I get or why hasn't anyone commented on my post? This can easily morph into self-doubt, leading to a downward spiral of self-criticism.

Have you ever had a meeting with your boss and walked away thinking "she hates me" or "he must think I'm stupid"? It's usually not because of something he or she said, rather something that was left unsaid. When you call a friend and leave a detailed message but don't receive a return call, what do you tell yourself? Maybe they're mad at me. What did I do to upset them? Did you ever stop to think that maybe the message accidentally got deleted? Or that they meant to call you back but life got busy and they simply forgot? Why do we assume it's all about us?

I'm notorious for falling into this thought pattern. I would often make up a terrible commentary in my head about some perceived injustice or why someone didn't respond to me. Despite receiving good employee evaluations, feedback, and promotions, getting an email from my boss requesting a call or meeting with him would immediately send me into a tailspin. I would begin thinking that I must have done something wrong. I could carry the made-up scenario all the way to getting fired. By the time I would meet with him, I'd be all worked up and anxious. Rarely did it ever turn out to be a negative conversation. What we tell ourselves can be brutal. Many times relationships are permanently damaged because, instead of talking to the person about a comment or lack of response, we assume it could only mean one thing and we react emotionally. Some people get very defensive and go into attack mode, while others blame themselves for whatever is wrong in the relationship or in the world.

In one of the self-development classes I took, I was engaged in a small texting group with four other ladies. We shared our stories with each other and became quite close. One day when I posted in our group, no one responded. I began to question why and started making up what could have happened. Just a day earlier, another lady had posted in the same group and was over-whelmed with support, so I reasoned this could only mean one thing—they obviously didn't really like me. When I voiced my concerned to one of the ladies in the group, she admitted that she had experienced a similar feeling and had worried that the rest of us had started a separate group without her. What in the world would make us think this way? I guess it's human nature, but stop for a moment and consider that you truly have no idea why a person has or has not responded in a certain way. Why do we instinctively make it something about ourselves? Think of all the things that could be happening to cause a person not to respond. Maybe they're sick, had a busy schedule, dropped their phone in the ocean, or simply forgot—the list of possibilities is infinite!

Through this intimate group where we boldly shared our insecurities and inner thoughts, I realized we're all nervous and unsure of ourselves. No matter how confident and bold a person seems, if you could look inside that person's mind you would see their insecurities and fears. We all have more in common than we realize. Next time someone takes a group photo, notice what you do. You immediately look for yourself in the picture. If you think you look bad, the picture is awful, right?

Now that I'm in the second half of my life, I'm learning to accept my imperfections and the circumstances I cannot control. Finding a way to accept situations and adjust expectations is crucial. Acceptance is freedom. We all know the serenity prayer, "God grant me the serenity to accept the things I cannot change, the courage to change the things I can and the wisdom to know the difference" (Sifton, 2003). Much of my life, I kept trying to accept things I hoped would change, when, like Dorothy in *The Wizard of Oz*, I had the power all along. Meanwhile, I continued doing the same thing but hoping for a different outcome. I have so many examples of this. The most glaring is, of course, staying in a miserable marriage and continuing year after year, trying to fix, change, and hope that it would improve. My yo-yo diet loop was another perfect example. I would go on a crash diet—I've tried them all—lose some weight and then go right back to eating my unhealthy ways. Toward the end of my career, my healthcare jobs were yet another example. I would take a difficult leadership role and work as hard as I could, only to be disillusioned and discouraged with the organization after a few years, then move to another. Each new position promised to be better than the last, and every one of them ended up more frustrating and more difficult than the one before. And, of course, my friend alcohol—yes, the wonderful substance that held all the answers. It has a way of making you believe that this time it will be different. Over the years, I changed my drink of choice, from spirits to beer to wine, thinking that would be the answer. I was drinking to celebrate victories, relieve a stressful day, and maintain my social life, but even when I knew it was no longer serving me, I kept trying to change it up and keep it in my life.

> "The definition of insanity is doing the same things over and over while expecting different results."

> — - ANONYMOUS

WAS I INSANE? Maybe. But at least I've stopped the insanity loop. I left that toxic relationship behind and have vowed never to let myself get stuck in a situation like that again. I acknowledge that I must burn more calories than I consume, and not all calories are equal. I said goodbye to my faithful companion alcohol and continue to work on accepting and being my authentic self.

If you are under forty and reading this, congratulations. So often, it takes nearly a lifetime to appreciate these truths. Regardless of where you are in life, now is the time to put yourself first and make the changes you can to be the best you can be.

READY TO QUIT

aybe you can relate to bits of my story or see pieces of yourself and your own struggles. No doubt your journey to this decision will be different than mine. If you are thinking about taking a break from alcohol, first of all, congratulations! It is a big step to even think about bucking society and giving up the booze. Lucky for me and you, we are not pioneers. There are countless others who have found a happier, healthier life that doesn't include alcohol. Today, if you decide to take a break from alcohol, you are simply joining the sober movement.

If you are a non-drinker or completely happy with your relationship with alcohol, feel free to skip this chapter. I realize that not everyone who drinks has a problem or issue with drinking. I am not suggesting everyone needs to become completely alcohol-free. I will admit it is by far the best for me, but we are all unique. Your relationship with alcohol will be different from mine. So, to you, every-once-in-a-while or take-it-or-leave-it moderate drinkers: good for you. I used to be quite jealous of this, but now I accept that my relationship with alcohol is not a healthy one and I am very happy to live without it.

On the other end of the spectrum, if you have a physical dependency on alcohol, you will need additional support to stop drinking. It can be extremely dangerous to suddenly stop drinking alcohol if your body is physically dependent. I will never forget working on the step-down unit at the hospital and having to hang a vodka drip on a patient I was caring for. He was being admitted for a heart condition, but to prevent him from going into delirium tremens we started an IV with a bottle of vodka. Alcohol withdrawal is a very serious medical condition and should not be a solo journey.

Now back to the whys. Take a moment to think about the reasons you want to stop drinking. What is motivating you to take this first step? Maybe it's your health, maybe your medical lab work has started trending the wrong way, or maybe you just can't reach your ideal weight. Maybe you've had one too many hangovers and are sick and tired of being sick and tired. Maybe you're looking at your children or grandchildren like I did and saying, "Will I be around to see them grow up? Will I have the energy to participate in their lives?" Maybe you just want to reduce your risk of cancer, give your liver a break, or save money.

Whys are personal. Yours will be unique to you, but it's important that you take a minute to determine what is motivating you to make this change. Some of you will have suffered financial or legal consequences due to your drinking. Others may have lost an important relationship or job. Maybe you've witnessed a family member or friend suffer or die from alcohol use and want to change your path. Whatever your why is, write it down. List as many reasons as you can think of. This is a great start!

Now, let's move to the commitment. I suggest you take at least a thirty-day break, but ninety or more would be even better. You can extend your challenge as you approach or complete your goals. Whatever your commitment is, write it down. It's kind of like a contract with yourself. You're making a commitment to yourself not to drink. No one will really know if you keep this commitment or not. **This requires honesty with yourself.** The good news is there doesn't have to be an announcement or confession. If you want to keep drinking, you always have that choice. This challenge is totally voluntary and completely up to you.

Here are some practical tips to get you going on your amazing journey. These are my top ten favorite tips to survive the first thirty days:

1. **Make the commitment to yourself.** If you drink at all, RESET and go back to day one.
2. **Get a sober tracker.** Download an app to count your days. Sober and Quit That are free applications that help you track your progress. Another idea is to print out a habit tracker or get a calendar so you can mark off or color in your alcohol-free days—something visible to aid your journey
3. **Read some quit lit.** Order a couple of books.

Some of my favorites are listed in the back of this book, but there are so many to choose from

4. **Write down why.** List all the reasons you want to take a break from alcohol. Your family, your health, or any other reason. It's important for you to write these down. If you begin to question or doubt your decisions, refer to these whys.

5. **Join a sober community.** You can find an online group like One Year No Beer, Arete Way alcohol-free club or an organization in your local community.

6. **Change your routine.** If every night at six you have a glass of wine, plan to do something different at this time. Exercise, walk, shower, take a class—anything that's not what you have habitually been doing. Get out of your drinking routine.

7. **Surf the craving.** Your body will continue to crave alcohol for a while. Recognize that these cravings will come, but they will pass. When you acknowledge you're experiencing a craving, accept it and wait for it to subside. You are stronger than your cravings—push through it with your favorite new activity.

8. **Play it forward.** This is one of my favorites. You want to have a drink—yes it will feel good for a few minutes, but then what? Will you be tempted to have another and another? How will you feel after you've had a few drinks? Resetting to day one, going back through the initial detox stage—is it worth it? For me, the answer is

always no, especially as you move into double-digit alcohol-free days.

9. **List 101 things to do instead of drink.** Get creative. You'll find my list below, but I would love to hear what new activities you discover with all your newfound time.

10. **Don't drink!** Don't worry about your diet. Focus on not drinking and, if it means you have a few extra cupcakes the first month or so, that's okay. Don't try to tackle a new diet, prepare for a marathon, and quit drinking alcohol all at the same.

To REINFORCE YOUR AMAZING DECISION, let me just list some of the wonderful benefits you will experience once alcohol leaves your body.

1. Better sleep
2. More energy
3. Hydration
4. Decreased fat in liver
5. Weight loss
6. Better memory and concentration
7. Healthier, better-looking skin
8. Improved sex life
9. Lower blood pressure and heart rate
10. Healthier immune system
11. Reduced risk of breast, liver, mouth, throat, and bowel cancer

12. Happier outlook on life

IT'S NOT JUST what alcohol does to your body. Alcohol also makes it more difficult for you to do the things you know are good for you like exercising and eating healthy meals. It's so much easier to just order a pizza or skip the gym after a couple of drinks. Still not convinced? Do a Google search on the benefits of quitting alcohol or reasons to stop drinking? The research is clear that this drug is toxic. And think about all the money you spend on alcohol. Alcohol is expensive, especially if you drink out at events and restaurants. Think about what you could do with all that extra money.

Maybe now is when I should go ahead and warn you about the wave of emotions and feelings you may have a week or so off the juice. I'm not the one to explain all the scientific reasons for this, but I can promise you: it's normal and it will pass. You may feel angry or sad, irritated or flat. I had tons of repressed guilt overwhelm me, and dealing with these raw emotions without medicating can be scary at first. But we adapt and, once we adjust, our concentration, reasoning power, and coping skills increase. I'm not saying that if you stop drinking your life will be perfect and all your problems will magically go away, but why not give this new lifestyle a chance?

Take a break for thirty, sixty, or ninety days and see how much better it will make you feel. You alone are in full control of how much alcohol you consume. Consider the benefits, even if you only commit to taking a break for thirty days once a year. Or maybe you just cut back to a couple of days per week. You decide what works for you. If you don't feel better, then by all means have at it. You'll always have the option to return to your current drinking pattern, no questions asked.

One of the things I love about life without alcohol is all the extra time I have. Here is my list of 101 things to do instead of drink.

1. Take a walk.
2. Drink a cup of tea.
3. Take a shower.
4. Weed your garden.
5. Hug a tree.
6. Listen to a podcast.
7. Hug somebody.
8. Pet a dog or cat.
9. Try a barre class.
10. Laugh out loud.
11. Do yoga (maybe even hot yoga).
12. Meditate or pray (try an app Calm, Headspace, or Balance).
13. Journal.
14. Sing a song.
15. Take a drive.
16. Ride a bicycle.
17. Volunteer.
18. Watch TV.
19. Drink a glass of water.
20. Have a mocktail or alcohol-free beer.
21. Do Zumba.
22. Phone a friend.

23. Look up healthy recipes to try.
24. Write someone a letter.
25. Take a nap.
26. Take a bubble bath.
27. Brush your teeth.
28. Go on a swing.
29. Get a pedicure or manicure.
30. Listen to music.
31. Clean a drawer or closet.
32. Do housework.
33. Plank for a minute.
34. Make a healthy treat.
35. Make a vision board.
36. Do a craft you enjoy.
37. Jump rope.
38. Put on lotion.
39. Play cards.
40. Color.
41. Explore essential oils.
42. Plant a flower.
43. Have sex.
44. Think about a time when you were really happy and enjoy that feeling.
45. Swim, ski, wakeboard, or surf.
46. Do the "Hokey Pokey."
47. Sit outside and notice the weather.
48. Look at photos.
49. Write down three things you're grateful for.
50. Go thrifting.
51. Visit a friend.
52. Wash your car.
53. Read a novel.

54. Google the benefits of not drinking alcohol.
55. Birdwatch.
56. Go bowling.
57. Plan a holiday.
58. Count the money saved from not drinking.
59. Eat an apple or other fruit.
60. Play with a child.
61. Look at the clouds in the sky.
62. Play it forward.
63. Send someone an encouraging text.
64. Take a course.
65. Get an accountability partner.
66. Chew ice chips.
67. Dance like no one is watching.
68. Try a POUND drumming class.
69. Bake muffins to share.
70. Learn a new language.
71. Go to the park.
72. Do a weightlifting workout.
73. Book a session with a life coach.
74. Light a candle.
75. Watch a Netflix series.
76. Lie on a Shakti mat.
77. Watch a sunrise or sunset.
78. Visit the seaside.
79. Vacuum your car.
80. Do squats.
81. Skip or hop.
82. Play a board game.
83. Smell some flowers.
84. Meal prep for the week.
85. Read quit lit (books about being alcohol-free).

86. Do an act of kindness.
87. Get a massage.
88. Research something interesting.
89. Do karaoke.
90. Plan a sober party.
91. Jog or run.
92. Stretch.
93. Play hopscotch.
94. Say or write some affirmations.
95. Make a smoothie.
96. Write a letter to your future self.
97. Go to a museum.
98. Post something uplifting on social media.
99. Clean out the refrigerator.
100. Drink a cup of kombucha.
101. Delete old emails.

BUILDING A FOUNDATION

*W*e need to give ourselves the best chance of being successful, reaching our goals, and being the best versions of ourselves we can be. When I was drinking, I never really felt great. I felt good some days, but it wasn't until the booze was completely out of my system that I realized how much better I felt without it. When I was younger it wasn't nearly as difficult to recover, but as I got older it became more challenging. Alcohol was not the only thing tripping me up. I didn't sleep well and I ate poorly. I would set goals for myself but then drink, eat bad, and not get enough sleep. Think about how an athlete prepares for an event. Many of them follow a strict regimen, monitoring their diet, exercise routines, and sleep patterns. They go to great lengths to be sure their bodies and minds are in optimal condition, so they have the best chance for success. We might not be training for an athletic event or contest, but considering we only get this one chance at life, taking care of ourselves sounds like a pretty good idea.

I use a mnemonic to help me remember: PRECANS. This system may work for you, or you may want to tweak it or make your own. What matters is having a way to check in with yourself and stay focused.

PRECANS is my acronym of prerequisites that focuses on the fundamentals in order to feel your best and meet your goals. Health and wellness are multifaceted. None of us will be perfect in all areas, but striving to maintain these areas will give us the greatest advantage.

PURPOSE AND PASSION
Rest and Recovery
Exercise
Connection (with family and friends)
Alcohol-free
Nutrition
Sleep

LET'S tackle each of the PRECANS one by one:

PURPOSE AND PASSION

What is your purpose in life? What are you passionate about? These are things we don't often think about. We are caught up in the day to day and rarely do we take the time to ask ourselves what we really want out of life. This is a very personal pursuit and something you should strongly consider. The best way to start here would be to simply review your values. What is most important to you? Some soul searching and time spent here may help direct you to your purpose. Maybe it's your greatest desire to be the best parent you can be. Maybe a close walk with God is your passion. Maybe you want to save the turtles.

I admire people who know what they want to do early on in life and pursue it. My stepson Paul, a Navy fighter pilot, knew at an early age what he wanted to do. He began preparing as early as middle school for his career. He sacrificed many of his Saturday mornings, getting up early and dedicating himself to the required years of training. I know physicians who knew as a child they wanted to be a doctor when they grew up and their focus never wavered.

* * *

"If you do what you love, you'll never work a day in your life" –
—Marc Anthony

I have met musicians who, despite financial struggles, dedicated their lives to playing music and doing what they love. We may only hear about the very few who actually become famous for their craft, but there are many artists making a living doing what they enjoy. Others keep their creative dreams and passions on the back burner while they pursue their day jobs and meet financial obligations.

There are many stories and examples of people that are born to do what they're doing, but I would say the majority of us are not that lucky. Many of us stumble through life not certain exactly what we want to do when we grow up.

I was in the work program my senior year of high school and assigned to a job in a physician group practice. It was a decent position but not one I particularly aspired to. Ironically, I ended up working in a similar setting nearly my entire career. Was working in healthcare my passion? For many years, I worked diligently to become skilled and educated in the healthcare industry. The more knowledgeable and proficient I became, the more entrenched I was. Before I knew it, thirty years had gone by and the only thing I knew was healthcare leadership.

Life takes twists and turns, and our path does not always lead where we expect. Our goals and desires can also change over the years. I think the COVID pandemic changed many of us in that respect. We were forced to evaluate what's really important. With things shut down, we all had the opportunity to think about our lives. Even when things got a little more normal, people were changed. Many of us became unwilling to accept stepping back onto the treadmill of our previous lives. We found creative ways to do more with less and restructure our priorities to avoid going back into the stressful rat race. This is one positive from the pandemic with millions of people looking at what's most important to them and reprioritizing their life goals.

I have reached a point in my life where I likely have less time left than I have lived. For me, it was time to reevaluate, but why wait until you're my age? My values became clearer over time. I wanted time over money and relationships over material goods. I'm passionate about my bliss beyond the buzz and love sharing what I have found. I love helping others set goals, discover their passion, and live healthier happier lives.

Ask yourself what you want to do with the rest of your life and start doing that today! How will you spend today? What will you focus on? What's important to you? Think about what you were drawn to as a child. What did you want to do when you grew up? Go back and revisit your creative desires. Now I'm not saying everyone should quit their jobs and start painting, but I do think we often push through our lives without thoughts of what makes us happy or brings us joy or what we are passionate about. You know there are many successful people who changed careers or started pursuing their dreams late in life. Duncan Hines started his culinary career at age fifty-two. Laura Ingalls Wilder wrote her first novel in her sixties.

If you haven't thought about your values, purpose, or passion, it's not too late. If you need some help, try writing. Writing can sometimes help release your inner thoughts. Try freeform writing all the values you can think of and then number them in order of importance. I often use a blank page in my journal to just write what I am thinking. I call it a brain dump and just write whatever pops into my head. It can be surprising what you find on the page.

At the very least, try doing more of what you love and makes you happy!

Rest and Recovery

I have to admit this is a tough one for me. It's hard to relax and just do nothing. I have often been called a "hard worker." I guess it is true. I tend to be a doer. When I'm at home, I always see something that needs attention. There's laundry, cooking, cleaning, dishes, yard work—always something that needs to get done. I realized when I quit drinking that it was hard for me to switch off. When I drank, after a couple glasses of wine or a few cocktails, I didn't seem to notice all the to-dos, or maybe I didn't care. Once I felt a nice buzz, it was easy to forget tasks and get down to drinking.

Today, thanks to technology, we're always connected. You can answer emails, work from home, and multitask. Corporate life comes with a nice salary but also a sense of never truly being off work. Often, deadlines and decisions couldn't wait until Monday and needed to be addressed after hours or on weekends. Who can get into the office earliest and who stays the latest? You're secretly rewarded brownie points if you answer emails fastest, especially if it was sent at 3 a.m. I had one boss tell me that eighteen-hour days were expected. It appears some people give one hundred percent of their time and energy to their position, but can they really? At what cost? For how long? Ever heard the term burnout? It's very common for physicians and healthcare workers. I'm sure it exists in a lot of industries.

What about lifestyle balance? That is a term recently introduced and thankfully the younger generation is considering that there are other options than working yourself to death. I found out the hard way that there's more to life than working and making money. If you sacrifice your family time or your health, will it really be worth it in the end? No one says on their death bed, "I wish I had worked more." Read the regrets of the dying and you will find material goods, money, and work usually don't make the list. I saw this with my mom and my sister, and the only things that mattered in their final days were relationships. Balancing making a living with self-care and spending time with our loved ones and friends can be challenging.

Physical and mental rest are both important. I think we all know that resting our bodies is crucial, but what about our minds? I know that, for me, this has been a real challenge. Do you want to slow down time? Sit for a few minutes and do nothing. Set a timer for ten minutes and just sit—no thinking or planning. There is a whole industry based on trying to get us to slow down and relax. I have a couple of applications on my phone that I use, Calm and Balance, but there are many others. Yoga is another great mind escape. I really enjoy hot yoga and yoga on the beach. Whatever it is that appeals to you, walking or sitting in nature, hugging a tree, strolling the oceanside, or finding peace on a mountain top, take some time to rest and recover. Stressors in life are nonstop and it is important to prioritize YOU. Losing yourself in something you enjoy like painting, writing, playing an instrument, or knitting can also be a source of relaxation. Tap into your creative side and think of something you liked to do when you were young. Maybe some sort of dance or singing or something you used to like to play.

Take a break from technology. How many times do you look at your phone in a day? The number might frighten you. While technology is neither completely good nor bad, we need to be mindful of how we use it. It is so easy to spend countless hours scrolling social media without even realizing it. Responding immediately to texts, emails, and alerts can keep your mind revved up and active. Try limiting your screen time and leaving your phone behind when you go out in nature. Taking a true mental break can be challenging. Smart phones have settings to turn off notifications, monitor screen time, and limit time spent on apps, so take advantage of them. At the very least, become aware of how much time you're spending on your phone. When I turned on my screen time tracking, I was shocked at how much time I wasted mindlessly scrolling. Manage technology and let it work for you. There are so many wonderful websites, YouTube channels and social media pages, but be diligent about what you view and how you spend your time. One of my clients started scheduling two hours per night without any devices. She said it has really changed her life. She now has more time for meditation, reading, and building relationships.

Try journaling. It doesn't have to be fancy, just consistent. You don't need a certain kind of notebook or formula, although there are a ton of good journals out there if you want some structure. I'll share my style with you, and you can try it, modify it, or use something completely different (see Appendix 4). I enter my days alcohol-free and my weight at the top. I write my personal daily affirmation:

- I am good enough.
- I am smart enough.
- I make good decisions.
- Where I am is where I need to be.
- I enjoy living a healthy, sober, active lifestyle.
- Life is good.
- I am grateful.

- God loves me.

I list my current goal, a bigger goal I'm working toward. I make sure that my goal is measurable and specific, with a timeframe for completion to keep myself accountable. I also list a couple other goals I'm thinking about focusing on in the future—these often change before they become my main goal. I list my PRECANS and rank them from one to ten. This helps me realize if I am low in one area or another and helps me maintain my foundation of self-care. I write my grand-babies' names and circle them with a heart, reminding me to pray for them. Then I finish with gratitude by writing at least three small things I am grateful for each day. I like to do the gratitude writing at night before I go to bed. And that's my journaling system.

It may not work for you, but I believe the act of physically writing these things down helps solidify my commitment to them. There is also what people call the Law of Attraction. I'm not a person who espouses the concept completely, but I must admit that I have seen it in action. When I bought a white Honda, I started noticing just how many white Hondas were on the road. Did more white Hondas suddenly appear after my purchase? No. I just became more aware. By writing down your desires and goals, it keeps them in the forefront of your mind.

* * *

"BY BEHOLDING WE BECOME CHANGED."
    —Ellen G. White

. . .

Exercise

Exercise used to be a dreaded but necessary evil for me. I knew that exercising was healthy, but I'd never developed the habit. As a child, I never played any sports and, in high school, I was the unpopular girl who sat on the side in gym class. I never ran or swam or did any type of activity for fun. I hiked a few times and took a few Jazzercise classes back in the day, but physical activity and exercise were not part of my daily life. I had never even once been a member of any gym until I was fifty years old. Somehow, during my lifestyle change on my weight-loss journey with my personal trainer, though, I fell in love with exercise. I think it's because of how it makes me feel. Perhaps with my addictive personality, I got addicted to the endorphins, but it's something I don't mind being hooked on.

My mood is so much better when I work out. The key for me was finding something I actually enjoyed. I'm not a runner, as much as I would like to be all about marathons and medals, but that's just not me. I've done a few 5Ks and they were all right, but what I enjoy more is Zumba, POUND, yoga, weight training, walking, and biking. If you don't like the exercise you're doing, it's going to be hard to stick with it. Now, I'm not saying that I love every workout, that I'm excited every time I go to the gym, or that I don't have to push myself to go to my Zumba class. Sometimes it's a struggle, but at the end of the day I do enjoy it. Try a bunch of exercises to see what's a good fit for you. Maybe swimming or rowing is your jam. Some people like barre or Pilates classes. Keep looking until you find something that excites you. Perhaps you would enjoy goat yoga, a trampoline workout, or skiing.

Remember, every class is different based on your instructor, so don't assume you dislike all yoga after a single class. If you can afford a personal trainer, I would highly recommend going that route. If not, there are tons of online programs and fitness gurus to assist you on your journey. Tell yourself a different story—right now! I always used to say to myself, "I'm not a gym person. I don't like exercise. I'm no good at sports." Guess what? I never was, but now I have a new script: "I enjoy living a sober, healthy, active lifestyle." I really do love the way it makes me feel.

* * *

"Whether you think you can or can't—you're right."

— - HENRY FORD

Another cool trick is this: on top of formal exercise classes or routines, think of all the things you do during the day and see how much activity you are getting that way. A few simple tweaks to your routine can add a lot more movement. If you're doing laundry, squat to get the clothes out of the dryer. It's better for you than bending over, and you get a couple of squats in. Take the stairs at work, park farther away from the store—there are so many ways to get in some extra steps and every one counts. Even shaking your legs and repositioning them counts as movement. I had a Fitbit for years and recently moved to the Apple Watch like everyone else, but whatever you prefer to use to track your activity and set some fitness goals will really help.

THIS TIP MIGHT SOUND HOKEY, but consider getting yourself some workout gear. Just putting on some tennis shoes and active wear can make a huge difference. Even if it's just one outfit, invest in a pair of workout pants or shorts and a top. I remember when I first started exercising, I wanted to fit in and bought myself a couple of workout outfits. It sounds bizarre, but to this day when I put on my gym clothes it motivates me. Whatever it takes, right?

I also want to give strength training a special plug here. Building muscle is very important. Unfortunately, as early as thirty years old, our bodies begin losing muscle mass. Sarcopenia is a condition characterized by loss of muscle mass and strength as we age. To avoid sarcopenia, it's necessary to stay active and to build and strengthen our muscles. Muscle loss causes weakness and can make daily task like getting up and down more difficult. It also increases the likelihood of falls and broken bones. Not to mention, it becomes even more difficult to build muscle after the age of fifty—not impossible, just more difficult. Staying active and lifting weights, or strength training, will be your best defense to maintain muscle strength. I'm not suggesting you need to be a body builder, but using dumbbells and weights or resistance bands can be beneficial. Be sure to get proper instruction and check with your doctor before starting any new fitness program, but please start one.

You may have heard the phrase "sitting is the new

smoking." In an article for the Mayo Clinic, Dr. Laskowski says the following:

> "Research has linked sitting for long periods of
>   time with a number of health concerns. They
>   include obesity and a cluster of conditions—
>   increased blood pressure, high blood sugar,
>   excess body fat around the waist and
>   abnormal cholesterol levels—that make up
>   metabolic syndrome. Too much sitting overall
>   and prolonged periods of sitting also seem to
>   increase the risk of death from cardiovascular
>   disease and cancer." (Laskowski, 2020)

A SEDENTARY LIFESTYLE is proving to be very bad for your health. If your job is computer based, consider a standing desk or at least one that is adjustable. There's so much information out there about simple, effective tips for increasing your activity level.

I wish everyone could fall in love with exercise, and I'm so very thankful that I did. Even if you don't love exercise, keep looking for an activity you like. We can't stop the aging process, but we can do our best to stay active and healthy. This is another point in my story where I want to say that *if I can do it, you can too*!

CONNECTION

I used to think this one was easy, because it comes natural to me, but I realize that connection is time consuming. When you are young and in school, making friends, hanging out, and socializing is all too easy. Taking the time to stay connected to friends and family is important. In middle age, as life becomes busier with our own family, career, and commitments, it is easy to ignore other relationships. Once we get older, we find many of our friendships have drifted away, even connections with our family members may have been put on the back burner. There are a couple valuable concepts I have found here. First, family is family, and you know what they say—you can't pick your family, but sometimes friends can become your chosen family. If you don't have a great support system in your family, you can focus on your family of choice. I am lucky to have a combination of both in what I call my inner circle. I have close relationships with some of my family members and some really close friends. If you have five or six people in your inner circle, you are blessed. Most people can't really maintain more than seven or eight within the circle. These are your people. These are the folks you call when something good happens to you. These are the people that you go to when something bad happens. They love you for you and have your best interest in mind. Some of you may only have one or two in this inner circle, and that's okay—the inner circle is more about quality relationships than quantity.

Once you realize these people love you no matter what, things become less important. Like whether you get the promotion or not. Your inner circle peeps love you even if you fail at something important, lose your job, or get fat. The inner circle has your back! Having a few trustworthy close connections is vital. It gives us the courage to go out into the cruel world. At the end of the day, these people are the ones that matter. Maintaining and nurturing these relationships is essential to your existence. If you have someone in your close circle that does not have your best interest at heart it can be dangerous. Fred as my husband should have been uplifting and supporting me as the closest part of my inner circle. Instead, he was constantly putting me down and belittling me. Removing him from my life was one of my greatest decisions. If you find yourself in close relationships with people who criticize and disparage you, end the relationship or at least set your boundaries. Life is hard enough without someone in your camp condemning or undermining you. You deserve to be supported!

The next layer of connection is more casual friends and family members. This group can be big. These are people you know and like, maybe even love, but they aren't necessarily in your inner circle of trust. This can be distant relatives you don't often see, your neighbors, or people you work with. This layer is also where you put your tribe, the group of likeminded people to support your endeavors. Like when I quit drinking, everyone in my inner circle still drank alcohol. I had to find a group of people who were with me on the alcohol-free journey. A tribe of people who understood my struggles and would be there to support me. It's not that my family and friends weren't supportive, but having people who actually know and understand what you're going through can be extremely helpful.

The thrivers and survivors of anal cancer from Blog for a Cure intimately understood what I had been going through during the merciless cancer treatment and they supported me in a way others in my circle weren't capable of. Both the sober group and the cancer group were online—I never would have thought that online relationships could have such an impact in my life. During the pandemic we found that Zoom, FaceTime, Skype, and other video platforms were the closest we could get to physically being there. Nothing replaces a hug, but we're lucky that we now can connect with people from all over the world. Finding a group that understands your unique struggles, even if it is online, can help.

As humans we need connection, and your health can suffer without enough of it. Love and belonging are listed on Maslow's Hierarchy of Basic Needs. If you have a good inner circle and a great group of friends, give them a hug, call them, and stay connected.

Alcohol-Free

I won't go over the benefits of being alcohol-free again, but I will say that once you have the experience for yourself, you will understand why I put so much emphasis on this and make it such a high priority. If you're an occasional drinker and alcohol is not a problem for you, then as they say, "If it doesn't apply, let it fly." But, if you have even one passing thought that you might drink a little more than you should, I invite you to give sobriety a try. The recommended amount of acceptable alcohol usage keeps going down. Some experts even say that "no amount of drinking is safe" (*Time*, 2018).

As part of the prerequisites of good health, it's just one less thing you have to compensate for. No alcohol means no extra empty calories. Your liver can do its real job and not work overtime trying to detox. I won't belabor the point here, since there is a whole chapter on it, but eliminating or at least reducing your alcohol intake is always an excellent idea.

NUTRITION

I will share what worked for me, but please do your own research and come up with a healthy diet that works best for you. I already told you about my personal trainer Darren and his famous good and bad lists (see Appendix 3)—eat stuff on the good list and don't eat anything on the bad list. In a nutshell, few carbs, no white potatoes or bread or pasta, nothing fried, no processed foods or sugary items, and allowed fruits are blueberries and grapefruit. On the good list are vegetables and meats. I call it The Darren Diet and have reverted to it and shared it with lots of people many times over the years. It's just basically a low-carb, low-sugar, clean-eating plan.

There are many other successful diets people enjoy like a plant-based diet, Keto, and intermittent fasting to name a few. I think I have tried them all. I tend to eat less meat than some, probably a leftover from my vegetarian days, but my "healthy" diet these days is a bit more relaxed, with some occasional cheese and a lot more fruit. I have added intermittent fasting several times a week, which just means not eating for twelve to sixteen hours after your last meal. If I eat dinner at 7 p.m., then I don't eat my first meal until 11 a.m. or even noon. The trick for me was finding a coffee creamer that didn't break the fast. I ended up switching to Nut Pods and that has done the trick.

I also want to address the importance of hydration

here. Drinking water is so important. I have a couple cups of coffee in the morning, but then it's just water for the rest of the day. You'll rarely see me without my water bottle. I think staying hydrated is one of the best tricks for healthy living. Not only does the body need and thrive on water, but it flushes out toxins. The bonus is the exercise you get making trips to the bathroom. My granddaughters are well versed in the hydration drill; it's a running household discussion about the color of urine, drinking enough water, and how to stay hydrated. It might sound a little odd but not unexpected when your grandma is a nurse. I would challenge you to try drinking a large glass of water as soon as you wake up in the morning (preferably room temperature). Then make it a point to stay hydrated throughout the day—don't wait until you're thirsty to drink water. Like I tell the kids, if your urine is not clear, you need to up your water intake. See what kind of difference this change makes. You can, of course, drink other fluids, but water is the king of hydration. Juices are delicious but full of sugar, and don't get me started on soda. Regular soda filled with sugar and diet soda filled with chemicals—just say no! Try to avoid or at least reduce the number of soft drinks you consume. As with everything, consistency is key. Healthy practices can become healthy habits and, the next thing you know, they're just part of your daily routine.

Finally, I want to touch on my nemesis—sugar. Sugar is the devil and continues to haunt me at times. Like alcohol, I tend to be "on the sugar" or completely off, because moderation is tough for me. Sugar is in almost everything. I try to eliminate or limit desserts, read labels, and avoid processed foods. I haven't had a soft drink in probably twenty years and only drink juices sparingly. I'm not saying you shouldn't have an ice cream cone or a piece of birthday cake, but it's surprising how addictive sugar can be. If you want to learn more about what sugar does to your body, I've listed some great books about it in the recommended reading list.

Sleep

Sleep is vital to all your organs. Unfortunately, though, getting a good night's sleep is not as easy as just lying down in bed. What do you need for a good night's sleep? A dark room, cool temperature, no distractions before bed, a sound machine, sleep stories, relaxation techniques, essential oils, and the ability to put the worries and cares of the day away.

Many books have been written on each one of these topics, so I won't attempt an exhaustive explanation of this topic. I'm just going to outline here what has helped me. I will say again, this is your journey, your one life, and you get to choose your own way. I am merely sharing some thoughts and ideas on what works for me in my journey toward my best life. Sleep is one of those must-haves for me. I simply cannot function without at least seven hours of sleep. I look back at my drinking days and wonder how in the world I managed to get by. My sleep pattern was one of the many things that pushed me to quit drinking. Waking up at three o'clock every morning with a racing heart is not conducive for a good night's sleep.

Even now that I'm no longer drinking, I still like to monitor my sleeping patterns. One way I stay in check is by journaling. As I rate and review my PRECANS, I become aware of which ones are slipping and may need a little extra attention. Maybe this week my sleep is suffering because I have some late-night commitments or stayed up late to watch a ballgame. I often struggle to get a good night's sleep when I'm out of town or have consumed caffeine after 5 p.m. Adding a nap is a great way to supplement sleep, if it's not too late in the day. I've never been much of a napper. I thought napping was for old or lazy people, but studies show just how beneficial naps can be. Napping can boost your mood, improve memory, reduce stress, and even help you sleep better. It's best to nap only ten to thirty minutes, since longer naps may cause you to be groggy (DerSakissian, 2020). While napping still isn't hugely accepted here in the United States, the evidence is clear that napping has excellent health benefits.

I love plopping down in my hammock on the lanai and putting on my nap app. Calm and Balance both have these types of programs. The narrator walks you through a few minutes of relaxation techniques, you drift off to sleep, and then a soft chime wakes you up after your allotted twenty-five or thirty minutes. It's quite refreshing and can make the rest of my day so much more productive. Despite this, I still don't tend to nap on a routine basis. I also realize most people work during the day and don't have this luxury. Americans in general pride themselves on working and undervalue rest, but maybe one day it will become more accepted, and we'll adopt the siesta custom like several other countries have.

. . .

PRECANS

PRECANS, not to be confused with pecans, is my secret weapon. On a daily basis, I use this mnemonic to help me focus on my overall health and well-being. I spend a few minutes scoring myself on a scale of one to ten in each category. Some days I may be a ten on nutrition, having chosen healthy meals and food prep. Other days I may score myself a three on nutrition if I ended up ordering a pizza out of convenience. Looking at my scores also gives me a sense of what area of my life needs a little more attention at any given time. The higher my score on these fundamental elements of life, the better I typically feel. I'll dive just a little deeper here into how you can set goals within PRECANS to help you measure your progress.

Purpose or Passion is a little difficult to measure, but they are important to keep in the forefront of your mind. Hopefully all the areas of your life uplift and support your passion. I rate purpose based on how aligned my day-to-day life is with my vision or the mission statement of my life. I strive to spend time with family and friends, stay healthy, and pursue my passion of helping others improve their lives. To determine my score, I ask myself some of the following questions: How have I spent my day? Did I have contact with my friends or family? Did I help anyone today? Was I calm and true to myself?

Rest and Recovery. It's up to you whether you want to score yourself daily or weekly. Ask yourself some of the following questions: Did I journal? Did I engage in something I enjoy or take a nap or meditate? These are questions I ask to help determine my score for this category.

Exercise is an easy one to rate and score. What are

your fitness goals? I usually have goals like ten thousand steps a day and strength training at the gym three times a week. Sometimes I change it up and add yoga or walking. Measuring and tracking activities make this one relatively effortless, but you might want to be sure you are challenging yourself and mixing it up to avoid boredom and complacency.

Connection is usually rated for me by how many contacts I have made. Planning time with friends or family visits, making calls, and staying in touch with people. You can set specific goals or just go with your gut on how connected you feel to your peeps.

Alcohol-free is a ten out of ten for me. I keep it on the list because it is a reminder, but if you are not alcohol-free you can still set parameters here to keep you accountable. Maybe your goal here is to only drink three times a week or to not have more than two drinks in a sitting. You can rate yourself based on your specific drinking patterns.

Nutrition is another area that can be tracked. Do you want to measure your weight gain or loss as your metric or get specific with calories? You can set specific goals for the number of days you want to fast or limit your sugar intake. The possibilities are endless with food trackers.

Sleep goals. Have you determined that you need eight hours of sleep or only seven? Maybe your goal is getting to bed at a certain time each night or getting up early. Again, you get to decide what you need for a good night's sleep.

Measuring PRECANS is not a magic formula and I have no doubt others have tackled the topic of being healthy in many similar ways. Maybe you are acquainted with the acronym HALT. It's a similar concept. If you're feeling Hungry, Angry, Lonely, or Tired, it's good to halt, or stop, and take care of that pressing emotion. Instead of correcting the underlying cause, we drink or react in a negative way. The term "hangry," which means irritable or angry due to being hungry, is now used to describe that common feeling. If we're not eating or if we're eating a crap diet of processed foods, sugar, and carbs, our fuse can become short and we may say or do things we wouldn't otherwise say or do. My good or bad days are typically dependent on these underlying principles. If I don't get a good night's sleep or I make some unhealthy choices at dinner the night before, it affects me the next day. Focusing on getting enough rest, exercising regularly, staying connected to my family and friends, remaining alcohol-free, eating a healthy diet, and getting enough sleep have made a huge difference in my life. You need to have awareness to make changes. Once you become aware and begin to focus on these principles, you can move toward making the necessary changes in your life.

"The thing that hath been, it is that which shall be; and that which is done is that which shall be done: and **there is nothing new under the sun**."

— - ECCLESIASTES 1:9

AFTERWORD

Happy Ending

"In the blink of an eye, things can change so forgive often, love with all your heart. You may never have that chance again."

— - UNKNOWN

I hadn't had a sip of alcohol in over three years. I was working out faithfully, eating healthy, sleeping almost eight hours a night, and my PRECANS scores were all pretty high. I was feeling good. My calendar was packed, then out of the blue, I woke up sick as a dog one morning. Headache, diarrhea, and overwhelming fatigue. I had no choice but to submit to bed rest. I could barely lift my head. Fever, chills, and short stints to the bathroom. I slept for more than twenty-two hours. As I lay there, drifting in and out of consciousness, I thought about how quickly things can change in life. I remembered my cancer diagnosis and how all my lofty goals and plans had been put on hold.

I was angry with my sickness. To make matters worse, I had an important presentation scheduled in a couple of days. I had been preparing for months, practicing and promoting. I was afraid I might have to cancel. But it wasn't up to me. The only thing in my control was how I responded to my sickness. Anger wouldn't help—it would only waste more precious energy. Rest, sleep, and fluids were the only real options. The next day when I woke up, I felt a little better. Now what? Should I rush back to my routine or take time to recover? I decided on the latter and spent most of the next day resting. Luckily the illness was relatively short lived and I was able to do my presentation. There have been some benefits to this pandemic, Zoom meetings from home being one of them, but it got me thinking about everything outside of my control. Honestly, there's very little within our control, but as I've said throughout this book, what we do have control over is our minds and beliefs.

Perhaps I'm a slow learner, but it has taken me almost sixty years to realize what I'm really seeking is contentment. I'm happiest when I'm enjoying what's happening now and where I am in the moment, including to some degree *who* I am. Instead of continually striving for the perfect waist size or social status, I'm taking life as it comes. It has always been difficult for me to rest in the moment. It still is. So often, instead of enjoying the present moment, I'm worried about the future, anticipating the next task—my never-ending to-do list—or less frequently regretting something in my past. My grandbabies have been extremely helpful in my journey to finding joy. Holding a sweet infant in my arms, getting lost in make believe, or playing with a toddler—it's moments like these that have a way of grounding me in the present moment. I realize how short these precious times are.

I was young when I had Jennifer and missed so many precious moments chasing trivial pursuits. I was entrenched in a horrible marriage, working full time, struggling to make ends meet, and my precious three-year-old wanting to play was often pushed aside or ignored. I had no way of knowing just how fleeting those years would be. I was too young and inexperienced to value the time. It went by so fast. I am so proud that Jennifer did not continue the cycle of abuse. She married Houston, a loving husband and doting father, and although not perfect, they have a lovely family. I am fortunate enough to be granted a second chance, if you will. I get to spend time with my granddaughters, playing, dancing, laughing, and cherishing every moment. There are still times I'm ready to give them back to their mom and dad, but for the most part the ever-present knowledge of just how quickly these years fly by is a constant reminder to enjoy every minute.

Did I find the magic key to happiness? Have I shared something in this book that will change your life and make you happy? Believe me, if it were as simple as writing a book and sharing my secret, I'm happy to do it. While I don't think I have a magic pill, I do wish that someone would have shared with me what I am sharing with you when I was younger. Maybe I wouldn't have listened or had the maturity to understand, although I like to think I would have. Whatever time of life you are in, now is the perfect time to be happy. So what's next? I'm free from toxic relationships and the stress of a traditional high-pressure job, my BMI is within a healthy limit, and I am alcohol-free. I'm enjoying eating a healthy diet and exercising, and for the first time in my life my self-esteem is pretty good. Let's say that I am happy being me.

What I realize in this chapter of my life is that I finally have a strong sense of not only who I am but of what I want to do. My to-do list and my goals are very different now as I near the sixty-year mark. I want—no, maybe it's more than want—I *need* to give back. In addition to spending as much time with my family and friends as possible, practicing self-care, and focusing on my PRECANS, I want to share what I have learned. Hopefully you will not spend twenty-five years in a toxic relationship or waste precious years numbing your feelings with alcohol. If this book helps one person move toward a better life, I've accomplished my mission.

Today I am a successful life coach. I work with people all over the world. My focus is on helping people meet their goals and change their lives. They are tired of not having a decent work-life balance and are sick of putting themselves last. Many of the women I coach are just like me and you. They are intelligent, giving, productive individuals that have raised families, pushed through to a successful career, and wonder on some level, "Is this all there is?" A life of accomplishments and successes but feeling a bit empty inside. Most of these ladies put a smile on their face and plod through life taking care of everyone around them—postponing their dreams as they fund their children's college, taking care of elderly parents, and doing what society expects of them. Unfortunately, many of these women have experienced sickness or catastrophic loss that have caused them to begin looking for answers.

Some of my clients have reached out because they didn't like how much they're drinking or how much they weigh. And nearly all of them, deep down, thought they were alone in this personal struggle. "I have a great family," said one of my clients. "A career, a house, and kids. I really have nothing to complain about, but . . ."

These wonderful ladies are not alone. In fact, almost every woman I have had the privilege of coaching has questioned even seeking help. Some of my male clients have similar struggles: providing for the family and attempting to live up to the masculine roles assigned by society. They share their lifestyle balance concerns and how alcohol has played out in their families and their daily lives.

The great thing about the coaching industry is that this is the plus side! Coaching starts at "I'm okay, but I just want to be better." Coaching is for anyone who just wants more out of life.

Having someone set aside time to truly listen to you and allow you the space and time to sort through your desires, goals, and limiting beliefs can seem indulgent. It's very sad that we can easily spend time and money on material items and anything the kids need, but self-development is rarely explored. What better gift can you give yourself and your family than to be the best version of you that you can be?

"Happiness Doesn't Lie at the End of the Goal Rainbow.
Happiness Lies in the Struggle, Not the End Result."

— - ANDY RAMAGE

My life is not perfect and I'm okay with that. My legs wrinkle up like an elephant when I do a downward dog. Dark sun spots dot my face. I still have a double chin and will probably never like my side profile pictures. But for the first time in my life, I am happy in my own skin. It's not about physical characteristics or beauty. It's about being healthy, fit, and thankful. I still have good days and bad days. Living a healthy, active lifestyle, focusing on my PRECANS, and trying to stay in the moment works for me most days, but I still occasionally get sick or worried or stressed. That is reality. As I put myself out there to share my story, I find not every client loves me and social media can certainly be brutal, but I must focus on the good and filter out the bad. Even in my own head. The key for me is gratitude—and I am grateful.

Thank you again for reading my book. If you are looking for encouragement and support to live your best life, please join me to find *your* bliss beyond the buzz.

APPENDIX 1

Suggestions for Further Reading

There are so many wonderful books out there, and this is by no means an exhaustive list, but here are some of my recommendations to get you started on your journey to bliss beyond the buzz:

Quit Lit

28 Day Plan by Andy Ramage
Alcohol Explained by William Porter
Drink?: The New Science of Alcohol and Your Health by Professor David Nutt
Quit Drinking Without Willpower by Allen Carr
The Sober Diaries by Clare Poole
The Unexpected Joys of Being Sober by Catherine Gray
This Naked Mind by Annie Grace

Self-Development

A Path through the Jungle by Prof Steve Peters

Atomic Habits by James Clear

Daily Stoic by Ryan Holiday

Eat That Frog by Brian Tracy

Essentialism: The Disciplined Pursuit of Less by Greg McKeown

Falling Upwards by Richard Rohr

Let's Do This by Andy Ramage

The Alchemist by Paulo Coelho

The Gifts of Imperfection by Brené Brown

The Kindness Method by Shahroo Izadi

The War of Art: Break Through the Blocks and Win Your Inner Creative Battles by Steven Pressfield

Abusive Relationships

Codependent No More by Melanie Beatty

The Language of Letting Go by Melanie Beatty

Women Who Love Too Much by Robin Norwood

PRECANS

Emotional Intelligence 2.0 by Travis Bradberry & Jean Greaves

Lagom (Not too little, not too much) by Niki Brantmark

Morning Magic by Arrmon Abedikichi

Strengths Finder 2.0 by Tom Rath

The Sleep Book: How to Sleep Well Every Night by Guy Meadows

The 7 Habits of Highly Effective People by Stephen R. Covey

That Sugar Book by Damon Gameau

When the Body Says No by Gabor Mate', M.D.

APPENDIX 2

Other Domestic Violence Resources

National Domestic Violence Hotline
1-800-799-SAFE (7233)
thehotline.org
P.O. Box 90249
Austin, TX 78709

National Coalition Against Domestic Violence
303-839-1852
ncadv.org
600 Grant, Suite 750
Denver, CO 80203

APPENDIX 3

The Darren Diet

The Good

- Almond butter
- Avocado
- Beef (Extra lean, grass fed)
- Bison (ground or steak)
- Blueberries
- Cayenne pepper
- Chicken breast (ground or whole)
- Cinnamon
- Coffee
- Cottage cheese
- Egg whites
- Fish (wild salmon, tuna, red snapper, mahi-mahi, halibut, sea bass)
- Flaxseed (ground)
- Grapefruit

- Greek yogurt (plain, 0% fat)
- Green or white tea
- Kale
- Legumes
- Lemon juice (fresh)
- Oat bran
- Oatmeal (steel cut or rolled oats)
- Quinoa
- Raw almonds
- Red bell peppers
- Skim milk
- Spinach
- Sprouted grain breads/wraps/English muffins
- Sweet potatoes (baked)
- Sun crystals/pure stevia
- Sunflower seeds
- Tomatoes
- Turkey breast (ground or whole)
- Vegetables (fresh)
- Wheat bran
- Wheat germ
- Whey protein powder
- Whole grain brown rice
- Wild rice

The Bad

- Anything fried
- Bread flour
- Butter
- Cereals
- Cheese

- Highly processed foods
- Juices
- Milk fat
- Partially hydrogenated oil
- Pasta
- Peanut butter
- Pork
- Pretzels
- Rice cakes
- Shortening
- Soda
- Sugar (high fructose, corn syrup, sucrose, dextrose)
- White grains

APPENDIX 4

Sample Journal

Date

I am good enough. I am
smart enough, I make
good decisions. Where
I am is where I need to
be. I enjoy living a
healthy sober lifestyle.
Life is good. . God loves
me. I am grateful.

Wt _____

AF Days _____

___ Purpose
___ Rest/recovery
___ Exercise
___ Connection
___ Alcohol Free
___ Nutrition
___ Sleep

Stretch goals
   Goal

Grateful for:
   1.
   2.
   3.

_____
timeline -
to - do's -
   1.
   2.
   3.

just write what you feel

BIBLIOGRAPHY

Bibliography

Blog for a Cure. https://www.blogforacure.com.

DerSakissian, C. (2020). *Health Benefits of Napping.* https://www.wedbmd.com/a-to-z-guides/ss/slideshow-health-benefits-of-napping.

Durcharme, J. (2018). *A New Study Says Any Amount of Drinking Is Bad for You. Here's What Experts Say.* https://time.com/5376552/how-much-alcohol-to-drink-study/.

Laskowski, E. (2020). *What Are the Risks of Sitting Too Much.* https://www.mayoclinic.org/healthy-lifestyle/adult-health/expert-answers/sitting/faq-20058005.

NCADV: National Coalition Against Domestic Violence. (2011). *Statistics.* https://ncadv.org/statistics.

Ramage, A. (2020). *Let's Do This! How to Use Motivational Psychology to Change Your Habits and Change Your Life.* New York: Aster.

Sarkis, S. M. (2017). *11 Red Flags of Gaslighting in a Relationship.* https://www.psychologytoday.com/us/blog/

here-there-and-everywhere/201701/11-red-flags-gaslighting-in-relationship.

Sifton, E. (2003). *The Serenity Prayer: Faith and Politics in Peace and War.* 6th ed. New York: Norton & Norton.

Tjaden, P., & Thoennes, N. (2000). *Extent, Nature, and Consequences of Intimate Partner Violence.* https://www.ojp.gov/pdffiles1/nij/181867.pdf.

ACKNOWLEDGMENTS

Thank you to all my friends and family, my OYNB tribe, Blog for a Cure, cancer fighters, my Full Potential Plan family, and The Arete Way coaching crew. Huge thanks to my therapist who is always there for me, letting me pop in for tune ups. Shoutout to all my Facebook peeps and all of the wonderful people I have worked with over the years. A deep heartfelt thanks and appreciation to my inner circle of family and friends, who have supported me through all my different careers, tragic events, phases, ideas, and dreams. You are the most important people in my life and I love you!

Thank you to Eric Romesburg and the ladies in my MBG group who read my book and gave me feedback. Y'all gave me the courage to keep moving forward with this project. Thank you to Paul Flagg, my editor who painstakingly redlined all my blunders. A special thanks to Dianne Farb, I could not have done this without you. Thank you for generously sharing your wisdom on writing, publishing and encouraging me throughout the process. Finally a huge thank you to Andy Ramage, who stepped out of his comfort zone and began his self-development journey—first with One Year No Beer and then The Arete Way. These programs changed my life. I will forever be grateful to you.

ABOUT THE AUTHOR

JANET FUGATE is a registered nurse and life coach. She is passionate about helping people live healthier, happier lives.

She has her masters degree in business administration and years of leadership experience mentoring and coaching. Janet lives in Florida and enjoys boating, shelling and sunsets. She is a devoted grandma and loves spending time surrounded by family and friends.

Janet indulges her hippy vibe with fun activities like interpretive dance, drum circles, singing, laughing and appreciating time in nature. She is always up to try a new type of yoga, exercise class or adventure.

Coach Janet uses "PRECANS" a system she has adapted to help monitor and evaluate key areas of her life and help her stay on track. Learn how you can use this method to improve your life and find your own Bliss Beyond the Buzz.

facebook.com/blissbeyondthebuzz
instagram.com/blissbeyondthebuzz

.

Made in the USA
Las Vegas, NV
23 August 2022